family circle®

D0433372

HOW TO COOK
Chicken

essential techniques,
classic recipes,
brilliant results

The Family Circle® Promise of Success

Welcome to the world of Confident Cooking,
created for you in the Australian Family Circle®
Test Kitchen, where recipes are double-tested by
our team of home economists to achieve a
high standard of success—and delicious
results every time.

MURDOCH
B O O K S

contents

how to use this book

How to cook chicken is divided into sections dictated by cooking method. There is a logical progression through the book, from basic stocks through to lighter cooking methods, such as poaching, steaming, grilling, barbecuing, stir-frying and pan-frying, then on to more hearty braised dishes, roasts and deep-fried favourites. The variations pages are there to encourage you to experiment with flavours once the basics have been mastered. Here's a quick guide to which cuts are best suited to these cooking methods.

Chicken cuts

Breasts – double or single breasts on the bone, skin on or off

Breast fillets – skin on or off

Drumsticks – the bottom part of the leg, skin on

Marylands – the whole thigh and leg, skin on

Tenderloins – sold separately or attached to the breast

Thighs – bone in, skin on or off

Thigh fillets – boneless, skin off

Wings – whole wings, skin on

Suitable cuts for cooking methods

For stock – Bones, necks, giblets, boiling fowls

Poaching – Whole chickens, breasts, breast fillets

Steaming – Breasts, breast fillets

Grilling – Butterflied chickens, halved or quartered chickens, breast fillets, wings, drumsticks

Barbecuing – Butterflied chickens, halved or quartered chickens, breasts, wings, drumsticks, Marylands, thighs, tenderloins

Stir-frying – Breast fillets, thigh fillets, tenderloins

Pan-frying – Breasts, breast fillets, drumsticks, Marylands, tenderloins, thigh fillets

Braising – Whole chickens, chicken pieces on the bone (breasts, drumsticks, thighs and wings), thigh fillets (when choosing chicken for casseroling, make sure it is plump and firm, but not too fatty, or you may end up with a pool of melted fat)

Roasting – Whole roasting chickens, baby chickens, wings, Marylands, drumsticks, thighs (when choosing a whole chicken for roasting, it is best if it is slightly fatty because the fat melts and prevents the flesh, particularly the breast, from drying out)

Deep-frying – All chicken pieces on the bone, breast fillets, tenderloins

The skin

A considerable portion of the chicken's fat is found in the skin. However, for those who are concerned about fat consumption, it does not matter whether you cook the chicken with the skin on or off, just as long as you don't eat it (this can be easier said than done as the skin is also one of the most flavoursome parts of the chicken!).

all about chicken

Readily available all year round, chicken is a wonderfully versatile ingredient. It is suited to a wide range of cooking methods, is mild in flavour, has a tender texture and is relatively low in fat. Chicken is delicious with the simplest of seasonings, yet can hold equally with the complexity of a robust marinade. On the following pages, we tell you everything you need to know about buying and storing fresh and frozen chicken, and give a step-by-step guide to jointing a chicken (both Western and Asian style).

Choosing the right chicken

Chicken is classified and sold by size and age rather than by breed. Whole chickens are labelled with a number which corresponds to their weight. For example, a number 14 chicken, aged 6 weeks, will weigh 1.4 kilograms, and will serve 3–4 people. Larger chickens, over 1.8 kilograms, have had time to develop flavour, however the flesh will not be quite as tender as a younger bird. Although they are fine to roast, they are more suited to slower methods of cooking such as poaching or braising. Poussin, also known as spatchcock, are baby chickens 3–4 weeks of age, weighing 400–500 grams, a perfect size for an individual serving. Whole chickens are often sold with the giblets inside the cavity, so check for them before stuffing or cooking.

Fresh or frozen?

Whenever possible it is preferable to buy fresh chicken rather than frozen. When the bird is frozen, the moisture forms ice particles which can pierce the flesh, and alter the texture, and may also result in a slight loss of flavour as the defrosting bird releases liquid.

Buying and storing fresh chicken

These days, there are many choices available to consumers regarding the size and rearing methods of chicken. However, for all chicken there are certain key points to look for when purchasing: it should have a light fresh smell; the skin should be a pale pink colour and moist, but not at all wet; the skin should be unbroken and free from blemishes and bruises; and the flesh should not have any dry patches.

Chicken should be transported home as quickly as possible. Leaving it to sit in the car will greatly increase the likelihood of rapid growth of harmful bacteria, such as salmonella, which can cause food poisoning. Keep fresh chicken away from any strong-smelling items, such as cleaning agents, as it will absorb the odour.

As soon as you get home, remove the whole chicken or pieces from its packaging, pour off any accumulated juices, and dry with absorbent paper. Remove the neck and giblets from a whole bird and store separately. Place on a plate, cover with plastic wrap and store in the refrigerator for up to 2 days.

Buying frozen chicken

When you are buying frozen chicken, make sure it is frozen solid, with the packaging intact. Avoid any that are softer and partially defrosted, or that appear to be sitting in their own liquid. If not using straight away, store the chicken in the freezer. Commercially frozen chickens can keep for up to 9 months, but it's always wise to check the manufacturer's instructions.

Freezing fresh chicken

Fresh chicken not being used immediately may be frozen. The freezer temperature should be −15°C or lower. Package the chicken securely, expelling as much air as possible (oxygen may cause the fat in the chicken to oxidise, and taint the flavour of the flesh). It is advisable to label the bags with the date, and also the cut of chicken if it happens to be in pieces or fillets. Cooked chicken may be frozen for up to 2 weeks — if you leave it any longer than this the texture of the flesh may start to dry out.

Defrosting safely

To defrost a frozen chicken, remove it from the packaging, sit it on absorbent paper on an uncovered plate and leave it to thaw in the fridge, allowing 2–3 hours for every 500 grams. The chicken should be cooked as soon as possible, and no later than 12 hours after thawing. Make sure it is completely defrosted before cooking, otherwise the uneven temperatures while the bird is cooking may cause the growth of the harmful bacteria salmonella. For this reason too, defrosting a whole chicken in the microwave is not recommended because of uneven thawing. Defrosted chicken must not be refrozen.

Keep it clean

Keep poultry refrigerated until you are ready to cook it. Avoid 'cross-contamination', which may encourage the development of salmonella, by keeping raw and cooked chicken completely separate, and always washing hands, chopping boards, knives and cooking utensils in hot soapy water after handling raw chicken. Never allow raw chicken or its juices to come in contact with other foodstuffs, particularly foods that are to be eaten raw.

Cooking a whole chicken

To prepare a whole chicken, remove the neck, giblets and any fat around the cavity. Gently pat dry and proceed with the recipe. If the bird is to be stuffed, make sure the stuffing is cold when placed into the cavity (the risk of salmonella increases if the stuffing is hot). Cook the chicken within 3 hours of stuffing it.

To test for doneness in a whole roast bird, insert a skewer into the thickest part of the thigh — the juices should run clear. Chicken should be cooked through, with no sign of raw flesh or pink juices. This is the only way to ensure that any bacteria has been destroyed.

A whole chicken may be easily jointed to give a range of different pieces (see pages 10–13), or they may be bought separately, on or off the bone, with or without skin. To test the doneness of a chicken piece on the bone, insert a skewer into the thickest part ensuring the juices run clear. If the chicken is a piece of boneless fillet, gently press the thickest part of the flesh which will feel springy, not soft when cooked.

Different rearing methods

The way a chicken has been reared and processed is a factor now affecting consumer choice. In general, mass-produced chickens are less expensive, they are reared on a large scale, and are freely available all year round. These chickens are fed pellets which speed up their growth, so they have reached a size where they are ready for the market within 60 days. As part of the slaughter process they are put in a bath of water and chlorine. This is to kill any bacteria that may be present, extend their keeping time, and to whiten the flesh. Chickens labelled as corn fed are also now produced

on a large scale. These chickens are fed pellets which contain 8–10% corn, which gives the skin and flesh a yellow tinge. Feeding them corn helps to break down tissue, thereby producing a more tender chicken.

Free-range corn-fed chickens are reared in a free-range environment and are fed pellets which contain corn.

Organic chicken, which tends to be at the more expensive end of the scale, has rigorous regulations which must be abided by in order to earn this label. The area in which they are reared has to have been free of pesticides for 5 years. For the next 2 years the soil undergoes tests to ensure there is no chemical residue. The food the chickens are fed must be certified organic, and the chickens themselves are reared outside in pastures which are rotated regularly to reduce the risk of health and environmental problems. These chickens, which have been allowed to grow at a natural rate, reach maturity at 98–112 days.

A note about cooking times

The difference in rearing methods affects not only the flavour of the cooked chicken, but the texture and the fat content. So depending on which type of chicken you choose, there may be variations in cooking times or a need for a temperature adjustment.

While testing the recipes in this book, we used a range of different chickens, and the cooking times varied considerably. Free-range and organic chickens tend to have larger meaty thighs which will take longer to cook through. It is important to increase the cooking times slightly to compensate for this, and be sure that the chicken is cooked through before being served. The meat will also contain more blood, as the flesh has not been bleached, and because of this may have a slightly pink tinge, even when fully cooked. For the sake of consistency, all the recipes were developed using mass-produced fresh chicken available in supermarkets.

Jointing a chicken in the western style

Learning how to joint a chicken is not a difficult process, simply requiring a cutting board, a sharp heavy knife or poultry shears, and a little patience. Often it can work out to be less expensive to buy a whole chicken and joint it rather than purchase the same weight of chicken pieces. You also have the freedom of choosing a corn-fed, free-range or organic chicken, which are generally only sold as whole birds.

The simplest method of jointing follows the natural line of the bird, and will give 8–10 pieces.

Put the whole chicken on a cutting board with the drumsticks nearest to you. Wipe with paper towel to absorb any moisture which may make the chicken slippery. Pull the leg away from the body, and cut through the skin and down through the flesh to the bone. Try to leave as much skin covering the breast as possible. Twist the leg to release the thigh joint at the body, then carefully cut around the joint to sever the leg.

Place the leg skin-side-down on the cutting board, and separate the thigh from the drumstick by cutting straight through the middle joint.

Push the wing down and away from the chicken. Cut through the joint where it is attached to the body, and repeat this on the other side.

Cut through the bottom of the ribcage to separate the breast from the backbone. Reserve the backbone for making stock.

Take the breast and lay it flat on the board in front of you. Cut down one side of the breastbone, and then down the other side. Remove the wishbone at the top wider end of the breast.

This will give you 8 serving pieces, or you can cut each breast in half across to give 10 pieces. Trim the pieces of any excess fat, and neaten the edges of the skin.

JOINTING a chicken yourself, rather than buying pieces, is not at all difficult. The simplest method of jointing follows the natural line of the bird and will give you 8 to 10 pieces.

A large, sharp knife, or poultry shears, and a sturdy cutting board are all the tools you need.

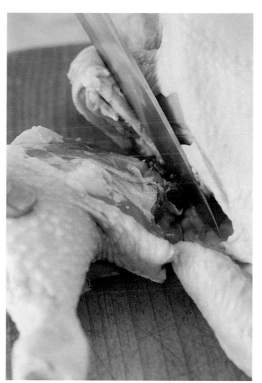

PAT the chicken dry, pull the leg away from the body and cut through the skin. Leave as much skin on the breast as you can.

FIND the middle joint and cut straight through it to separate the thigh from the drumstick.

PUSH the wing down, pull it away from the body of the chicken and cut through the joint.

CUT through the base of the ribcage to separate the breast from the backbone. Reserve the backbone for making stock.

PUSH the breast out as flat as you can and cut down one side of the breastbone, then the other side.

JOINTING A CHICKEN WESTERN STYLE 11

CLEAVERS have a rigid, thick blade, tapering to a sharp edge. They are perfect for jointing.

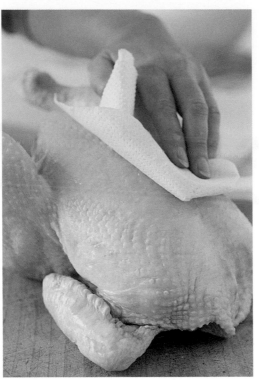

PAT all the moisture off the chicken, using paper towels, so that you can handle it easily without it slipping around.

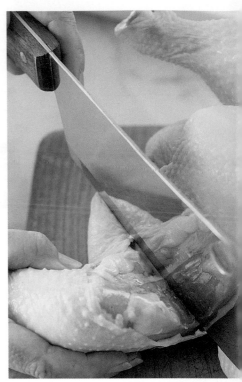

PUSH the leg and thigh away from the body, then cut through the skin. Twist the leg and thigh away.

PUT a leg down on the board and chop it into 5 similar-sized pieces. Repeat with the other leg.

PLACE a wing on the board and use the cleaver to chop it into 3 pieces. Repeat with the other wing.

CUT through the ribs to separate the breast from the back, then cut the breast down the middle.

Jointing a chicken in the asian style

Chickens jointed in this way are cut through the bone into bite-sized pieces. For this you will require an Asian-style cleaver and a heavy wooden chopping board.

Lay the chicken in front of you, and dry with paper towel. Remove the leg by pushing away from the body and cutting through the skin. Twist the leg to release the thigh joint at the body, and cut around it. Lay the leg flat on the board and chop decisively down into 5 pieces. Cut the pieces through the bone, but not through the joint. Wipe the ends of the bone with paper towel to remove any splintered bone.

Push the wing away from the body, and cut around the joint away from the body. Lay it flat on the board and chop it into 3 pieces, through the bone, but not through the joint.

Separate the breast from the back by cutting through the ribs. Cut the breast down the middle, on the side of the breastbone. Lay the breast flat on the board and chop each one into 3 pieces.

Rather than discarding the chicken carcass, neck and giblets, use them for making stock. The neck and giblets will add extra flavour. Or, if you prefer, freeze them for later use. Place them in a freezer bag, expelling any air, then seal, date and label and freeze for up to 3 months.

ASIAN cooking is often done quickly over high heat, so a chicken is usually cut into smaller pieces than for other cooking methods. It also makes eating with chopsticks easy.

White chicken stock

Home-made stock has a much better flavour than bought granules, cubes or tetra packs. This stock can be used as a soup base, for delicate sauces, and for poaching.

1.5–1.8 kg chicken
1 onion, roughly chopped
1 leek, roughly chopped
1 carrot, roughly chopped
1 celery stick, roughly chopped
2 bay leaves
6 black peppercorns
1 large sprig of fresh thyme

1 WASH the chicken inside and out, then place in a large saucepan or stockpot with the remaining ingredients. Pour in 3.5 litres of cold water and slowly bring to the boil.

2 SKIM off any scum that rises to the surface, using a skimmer or slotted spoon. As soon as the stock comes to the boil, reduce the heat and let it simmer very gently for about 1 1/2 hours. Don't boil the stock or it will turn cloudy.

3 LEAVE the stock to cool slightly before you strain it through a large colander to separate the chicken and vegetables from the liquid. Next, strain the liquid through a fine sieve to remove any bone, vegetable and herb fragments. The chicken can be eaten while still warm, or cooled completely, then refrigerated for later.

4 ALLOW the stock to cool completely before refrigerating it overnight. The next day, spoon off the layer of fat that has formed on top, and the stock is ready to use.

MAKES 3.25 litres.

SERVE the warm chicken meat with some hollandaise or pesto for a delicious lunch, or refrigerate it to use later in pasta dishes, sandwiches and salads.

STOCK will keep in the refrigerator for 3–4 days, or can be frozen for up to a month. Freeze it in plastic containers in usable quantities of 250 ml or 500 ml.

USE this stock, as well as the chicken, for the Chicken and vegetable soup on page 20.

WHITE chicken stock is light in colour and has a delicate flavour. Brown stock (see page 16) is dark and has a more robust flavour because of the roasted bones and vegetables.

DON'T add salt to the stock as the stock will be used in all types of recipes and the seasoning should be adjusted for each individual dish.

IT is important to skim off as much fat and scum as possible as it rises to the surface. Also, remove all visible fat before straining the stock.

USE a fine sieve to remove any sediment left after the first straining. Strain into a heatproof bowl and cool to room temperature before refrigerating.

SPOONING off the layer of fat that has formed after refrigeration is the final step in ensuring a clear and flavoursome stock with a low fat content.

THE richness of this stock is achieved by first roasting the ingredients until golden. You can buy chicken bones from poultry shops and butchers.

TRANSFER all the contents of the roasting tin to the stockpot. Don't add salt as this stock will be rich and flavoursome as it is.

DEGLAZE the pan by scraping off any of the stuck-on crusty remnants with wine, a little water and a wooden spoon. Add this to the stockpot for extra flavour.

STRAINING the stock will ensure that any sediment is removed. Strain it through a colander first, then strain the liquid through a fine sieve.

AFTER removing the fat, you can use the stock straight away for soups or return it to a clean pan and reduce it by half for sauces.

Brown chicken stock

This stock, with its robust flavour, is used mainly for making clear soups such as consommé and in sauces which require richness and a deep colour.

1 kg chicken bones
500 g chicken wings
1 tablespoon olive oil
2 brown onions, unpeeled
2 carrots, roughly chopped
2 celery sticks, roughly chopped
1 large tomato, roughly chopped
1 cup (250 ml) dry white wine
2 bay leaves
2 sprigs of fresh thyme

1 PREHEAT the oven to hot 220°C (425°F/Gas 7). Put the bones and wings in a large roasting tin, drizzle with half the oil and roast for 30 minutes. Add the vegetables, toss them in the remaining oil and continue cooking for 30 minutes, or until the vegetables are golden brown. If the tips of the bones darken too quickly, cover them with foil.

2 USE tongs to transfer all the bones and vegetables to a large stockpot. Pour the white wine and 1 cup (250 ml) of water into the tin, place on the heat and bring to the boil, scraping up all the brown, crusty bits from the base. Pour this into the stockpot. Cover with boiling water, add the herbs and bring slowly to the boil. Using a slotted or metal spoon, skim the scum from the top of the stock and discard. Reduce the heat and simmer gently for 1 1/2 hours. Don't boil the stock.

3 STRAIN the stock through a colander, discard all the bones and vegetables, then strain the liquid through a fine sieve to remove any bone, vegetable and herb fragments. Allow the stock to cool, then refrigerate it overnight. The next day, spoon off the layer of fat that has formed on top of the stock. If you want to use it straight away for saucing or glazing, return the stock to a clean pan and reduce it to half its original quantity (this concentrates the flavour). Otherwise, refrigerate it for 3–4 days, or freeze it for up to a month, in usable quantities.

MAKES 2.5 litres.

Chicken consommé

The name for this clear soup comes from the French *consommer,* meaning 'to use up'. It is so called because all the goodness of the chicken goes into the liquid.

1 small chicken breast fillet (about 100 g), roughly chopped
2 egg whites (don't discard the shells)
1.25 litres brown chicken stock from page 16

1 PUT the chopped chicken breast in a food processor and process it until it is finely chopped.

2 WHISK the egg white in a bowl until it froths, then add the minced chicken. Crush the egg shells, add to the bowl and stir until they are well mixed in.

3 SPOON away the layer of fat from the brown chicken stock, then pour the stock into a large saucepan. Add the chicken, shell and egg white mixture and just bring the stock to the boil. Reduce the heat and simmer for 25 minutes. During this time, all the impurities in the stock will adhere to the eggshell 'raft'. Don't let the stock boil or it will turn cloudy.

4 SET a large sieve over a bowl and line it with muslin or cheesecloth. Pour the stock through the lined sieve (the stock should be rich and clear). Discard the eggshell mixture. Season to taste with salt and white pepper.

SERVES 4.

To make traditional garnishes for consommé:

POACH quail eggs and serve in individual bowls of consommé.

CUT fine julienne strips of leek, carrot and celery and blanch them in the consommé.

CUT small threads of vermicelli pasta and cook them separately before serving in the consommé.

CONSOMME is delicious as a first course. If you want to garnish it, and add a little more texture and flavour at the same time, blanch some finely julienned vegetables in it.

IF you don't have a food processor, you can chop the chicken with a knife. Chop it very finely to make sure an even raft forms on top of the consommé.

EGG whites set when they are heated in the stock. Together with the chicken and eggshell, they form the clarification mixture for this consommé.

THE clarification mixture is used in consommés to catch impurities as they rise to the top. They cling to the raft, resulting in a perfectly clear soup.

TO ensure you end up with a completely clear consommé, use muslin as a filter to remove any remaining very fine particles of sediment and fat.

WHEN the stock has rested overnight in the refrigerator, the fat will rise to the top and set. This makes it easy to spoon off.

THE extra time needed for cooking the root vegetables also allows a rich flavour to develop. Experiment with sweet potato or pumpkin.

YOU can use other quick-cooking vegetables, such as fresh corn and zucchini, when you add the peas and beans.

CHICKEN flesh cooked while making a stock has a delicious flavour because of the long, slow cooking with herbs and vegetables.

Chicken and vegetable soup

This soup makes the most of a whole chicken. The flavour from the skin and bones is extracted while making the stock and the flesh is added to the soup.

3.25 litres white chicken stock from page 14
  (reserve the chicken flesh)
1 large potato, cut into 2 cm cubes
2 carrots, sliced into rounds
1 large leek, sliced
100 g shelled peas
100 g green runner beans, trimmed
  and cut into 2 cm lengths
small pinch of cayenne pepper, optional
3 tablespoons chopped fresh parsley

1 SPOON away the layer of fat from the surface of the stock, then bring the stock to the boil in a large saucepan. Reduce the heat, then add the potato, carrot and leek to the stock and simmer for 10 minutes, or until the vegetables have softened. Add the peas and green beans, then simmer for another 15 minutes.

2 PULL the skin off the chicken, then tear the flesh from the bones and cut it into bite-sized chunks. Add the chicken to the soup, along with the cayenne pepper, and season well with salt and freshly ground black pepper. Simmer the soup for 10 minutes, or until the chicken is warmed through. Stir in the parsley just before serving.

SERVES 4–6.

THIS soup makes a hearty meal. You can vary the flavour by using seasonal vegetables and herbs. Perhaps instead of adding parsley, you can serve it with a dollop of pesto.

Chicken and corn soup

This delicious, hearty soup has a sweetness that comes from the combination of both the corn kernels and the creamed corn.

3 cups (750 ml) white chicken stock from page 14

2 chicken breast fillets (about 200 g each)

3–4 corn cobs

1 tablespoon oil

4 spring onions, thinly sliced, greens chopped
   and reserved for garnish

1 clove garlic, crushed

2 teaspoons grated fresh ginger

310 g can creamed corn

1 tablespoon Chinese rice wine

2 tablespoons light soy sauce

1 tablespoon cornflour

2 teaspoons sesame oil

1 PLACE the stock in a saucepan and bring to the boil. Add the chicken, cover and remove the pan from the heat. Allow the chicken to cool in the liquid. Remove the chicken with a slotted spoon, then finely shred the meat using your fingers.

2 CUT the corn kernels from the cobs to yield about 2 cups (400 g). Heat the oil in a heavy-based saucepan or wok and add the spring onion, garlic and ginger. Stir for 30 seconds, then add the stock, corn kernels, creamed corn, rice wine and soy sauce. Stir until the soup comes to the boil, then reduce the heat and simmer for about 10 minutes. Add the chicken meat.

3 STIR the cornflour, sesame oil and 1 tablespoon water together in a small bowl until smooth. Add a little of the hot stock, stir to blend, then pour this mixture into the soup. Bring to simmering point, stirring constantly for 3–4 minutes, or until slightly thickened. Taste and, if necessary, adjust the seasoning. Garnish with the chopped reserved spring onion.

SERVES 4.

IF fresh corn cobs are not in season, you can use 2 cups (400 g) of drained, canned corn kernels, or the same amount of frozen corn kernels.

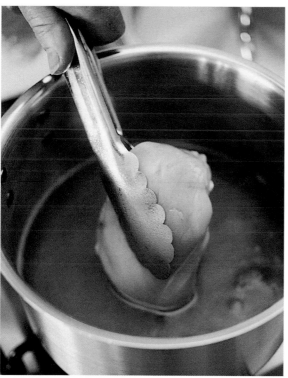

THIS gentle Asian-influenced poaching technique ensures that the chicken is tender, moist and full of flavour from the stock.

AS soon as the liquid starts to boil, the heat is reduced to very low so that the soup can cook but still retain the texture of the corn kernels.

CORNFLOUR is mixed with the sesame oil and water to form a 'slurry' which is stirred into the soup to thicken it.

TO make a slight variation to the soup, add some gently broken-up dried egg noodles about 5 minutes before the end of the cooking time.

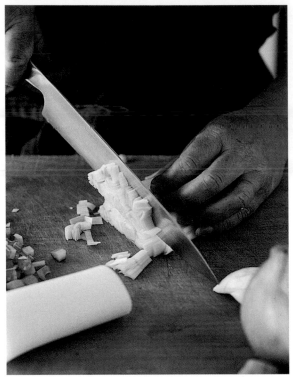

USING pale-coloured vegetables and not allowing them to caramelise during the cooking process ensures a fresh, creamy appearance.

THE plain flour is 'cooked out' for 5 minutes to ensure that the flour thickens the soup but does not add an undesirable floury flavour.

STIRRING constantly while adding the stock helps to emulsify the soup and attain the smooth texture that makes this soup so appealing.

IF you prefer a less rich soup, or are watching your fat intake, leave out the cream and add an extra ½ cup (125 ml) of stock. It will still be delicious.

INSTEAD of a chive garnish, make croutons with day-old bread. Remove the crusts, cut the bread into cubes and fry in hot oil, with garlic cloves if you like. Toss until brown.

Cream of chicken soup

This is a velvety, smooth soup that is perfect to serve as a first course at a dinner party, or to have as a delicious light supper or a warming lunch.

100 g butter
1 onion, finely diced
2 cloves garlic, crushed
1 leek, white part only, finely chopped
2 celery sticks, finely chopped
200 g chicken breast, cut into 1 cm dice
1/4 cup (30 g) plain flour
1 litre white chicken stock from page 14
1/2 cup (125 ml) cream, plus 2 tablespoons, for serving
2 teaspoons finely chopped fresh chives, for serving

1 MELT the butter in a heavy-based saucepan over low heat, then add the onion, garlic, leek and celery. Sauté, stirring frequently so that the vegetables don't brown at all, for 15 minutes (slowly and gently sautéeing the vegetables at this stage allows their flavours and sweetness to develop).

2 ADD the chicken to the pan and cook, stirring occasionally, for 5 minutes. Add the flour and stir to combine thoroughly over the heat. Cook for 5 minutes, then slowly add the chicken stock, a little at a time, stirring well so that lumps don't form.

3 BRING to simmering point, then cook, uncovered, for 30 minutes. Allow to cool slightly before blending in batches until quite smooth. It is important to allow the soup to cool before putting it in the blender, as the pressure when the soup is hot may cause the blender lid to come loose and allow the soup to splatter. Pour the soup back into a clean saucepan, add the cream, then bring back to a simmer and season to taste.

4 POUR into serving bowls, swirl about 2 teaspoons of the extra cream through the middle of each bowl of soup, then scatter with chopped chives.

SERVES 4.

Chicken gumbo

Gumbo is a complex, hearty, soupy stew that has traditions firmly rooted in New Orleans, Louisiana, USA.

1/3 cup (80 ml) vegetable oil
1/4 cup (30 g) plain flour
600 g chicken thigh fillets
60 g unsalted butter
100 g smoked ham, diced
150 g chorizo, thinly sliced
2 onions, chopped
2 cloves garlic, finely chopped
2 celery sticks, finely sliced
1 red capsicum, finely chopped

450 g tomatoes, peeled, seeded
    and chopped
2 cups (500 ml) white chicken
    stock from page 14
1 bay leaf
2 teaspoons fresh thyme
Tabasco, to taste
350 g okra, cut into 1 cm slices
2 spring onions, sliced, to garnish
2 tablespoons chopped fresh
    parsley, to garnish

1 HEAT 3 tablespoons of the oil in a small heavy-based saucepan, add the flour and stir to make a smooth paste. Stir over very low heat for 1 hour, or until the roux turns very dark brown, but is not burnt. This requires a great deal of patience and stirring but provides the gumbo with its dark look and rich flavour — the roux should be the colour of dark chocolate. Remove from the heat.

2 PAT dry the chicken thigh fillets with paper towels, cut into quarters and lightly season with salt and pepper. Heat the remaining oil and half the butter in a heavy-based frying pan over medium heat. Cook the chicken for 5–6 minutes, or until golden brown. Remove the chicken with a slotted spoon. Add the ham and chorizo and cook for another 4–5 minutes, or until lightly golden. Remove, leaving as much rendered fat in the pan as possible.

3 ADD the remaining butter to the same pan and cook the onion, garlic, celery and red capsicum over medium heat for 5–6 minutes, or until the vegetables have softened. Transfer the vegetables to a heavy-based, flameproof casserole. Add the tomato and the roux to the vegetables and stir well. Gradually stir the stock into the pan. Add the herbs and season with the Tabasco. Bring to the boil, stirring constantly.

4 REDUCE the heat, add the chicken, ham and chorizo to the casserole and simmer, uncovered, for 1 hour. Add the okra and cook for another hour. Skim the surface as the gumbo cooks because a lot of oil will come out of the chorizo. The gumbo should thicken considerably in the last 20 minutes as the okra softens. Remove the bay leaf and serve the gumbo in deep bowls. Garnish with spring onion and parsley.

SERVES 4.

IF refrigerated overnight, gumbo will thicken quite a bit so, when reheating, thin it by adding a little stock or water.

IF you are not a fan of the viscose texture caused by okra, try frying it in a little oil for 10 minutes, then add to the gumbo in the last 15 minutes.

TRADITIONAL gumbo uses an oil roux base which adds a rich colour and flavour to the dish and also helps to thicken the liquid.

CHORIZO is a spicy Spanish sausage best known for its use in paella. It is most commonly made from pork (or pork and beef) and red capsicums.

FOR a delicious seafood variation, try adding some shelled green prawns with the tails intact or shelled oysters at the end of cooking.

The perfect poached chicken breast

Poaching is a light, healthy and flavoursome method of cooking. Poached chicken breast is delicious served with a simple sauce or can be used in the salads on the following pages.

3 cups (750 ml) white chicken stock from page 14, lightly seasoned
4 chicken breast fillets, skin removed

1 POUR the stock into a saucepan and bring to the boil. Remove from the heat, add the chicken to the stock, then cover and allow to cool in the liquid. After about 10 minutes, the chicken should be cooked (this time may vary by 1–2 minutes, depending on the size of the breasts). Test by touching with your finger — the chicken should feel quite springy.

2 BE careful not to allow the chicken to boil in the liquid or it will become tough and dry.

3 IF you want to serve the chicken warm, cook it just prior to eating — it will dry out if reheated. Cut the breast on the diagonal, drizzle with one of the sauces on the facing page and serve with a fresh green salad. A perfect light lunch.

4 FOR cold dishes, the poaching can be done up to a day in advance. To prevent the chicken from drying out, store it in the cooking liquid, in the fridge, until you are ready to use it. Turn the page for some lovely suggestions for poached chicken salads.

SERVES 4.

IF you are making an Asian-flavoured dish, add aromatics such as garlic, star anise, ginger, fresh coriander and kaffir lime leaf to the stock. You can also poach the chicken in coconut milk or a combination of coconut milk and stock.

IF the flesh feels very soft to the touch, it is not quite cooked. Return the chicken to the poaching liquid for a few minutes or longer, depending on the size of the breasts.

Aïoli

4 cloves garlic
2 egg yolks
1¹/₄ cups (315 ml) light olive oil
1 tablespoon lemon juice
pinch of ground white pepper

COMBINE the garlic, egg yolks and a pinch of salt
in a food processor and process for 10 seconds.
With the motor running, add the oil in a thin, slow
stream. When the mixture starts to thicken, you can
add the oil a little faster. Process until all the oil
is incorporated and the aïoli is thick and creamy.
Stir in the lemon juice and pepper. Taste and add
more salt if necessary.

MAKES 1¹/₂ cups.

Salsa verde

1 tablespoon capers in salt
2 cloves garlic
6 anchovy fillets
40 g fresh parsley
20 g fresh basil
20 g fresh mint
1 teaspoon Dijon mustard
1 tablespoon red wine vinegar
¹/₂ cup (125 ml) olive oil

RINSE the capers and pat dry with paper towels.
Roughly chop the capers, garlic and anchovies,
place in a food processor with the herbs and
process until finely chopped. Mix in the mustard
and red wine vinegar, then slowly add the olive oil,
a little at a time. Season, to taste, with sea salt and
freshly ground black pepper.

THIS sauce is best made and used on the same day
as it tends to lose its fresh flavour after 24 hours.

MAKES ³/₄ cup.

The perfect steamed chicken breast

Steamed chicken breast has unlimited uses. Not only is it excellent for salads or light meals, it works wonderfully served whole with Asian sauces, as shown on the next page.

2 cups (500 ml) white chicken stock from page 14
3 cm x 2 cm piece of fresh ginger, finely sliced
1 clove garlic, finely sliced
4 chicken breast fillets (about 200 g each), skin removed, trimmed

1 POUR the stock into a wok. Add the ginger and garlic, bring to the boil, then reduce the heat to low. Simmer gently for 5 minutes to allow the flavours to infuse.

2 LIGHTLY season the chicken breasts with salt and freshly ground black pepper. Line a bamboo steamer basket with baking paper and place the chicken breasts on the paper, making sure the breasts aren't touching one another. Depending on the size of your steamer basket, you may need two steamer trays, or you may need to cook the breasts in two batches. If you don't have a wok and bamboo steamers, you can use a saucepan and place a metal steamer tray over it.

3 COVER the steamer and place it over the wok for 10 minutes, or until the breasts are cooked through. To test, touch the chicken to see if it is springy. Remove from the steamer, transfer to a plate and cover with foil for 3 minutes (leaving the chicken to rest allows the flesh to relax, resulting in tender and moist chicken). Slice the breast across the grain and serve with jasmine rice and a green salad, or with one of the Asian sauces on the following pages.

SERVES 4.

ALLOW the aromatics to simmer for 5 minutes before adding the breasts so the liquid is infused and the steam carries the flavour to the chicken.

LINING the bamboo steamer basket with baking paper ensures that the chicken breast won't stick to the steamer. It also makes it easy to lift it out.

CUTTING the chicken across the grain of the flesh helps with tenderness because you are cutting through the connective tissue, instead of along it.

WHEN the chicken is cooked, it will feel springy when pressed. If it feels very soft to the touch, it is not quite cooked. Return the chicken to the steamer and cook for another few minutes.

TRY adding other aromatics to the steaming liquid. Kaffir lime leaves, lemon grass or chillies would all give their own distinctive flavours.

asian sauces for steamed chicken

ginger and spring onion

SCATTER 2 teaspoons finely julienned fresh ginger and 2 tablespoons finely sliced (on the diagonal) spring onion over 4 steamed, hot chicken breasts. Pour 2 tablespoons soy sauce over them. In a small pan, heat 2 tablespoons peanut oil and $1/2$ teaspoon sesame oil until hot, but not smoking. Carefully spoon the oil over the chicken and serve immediately.

chilli bean sauce

IN a small saucepan, mix together $1/3$ cup (90 g) yellow soy bean paste, $2^1/2$ teaspoons sugar, $1/4$ cup (60 ml) chicken stock, $1/4$ teaspoon crushed garlic and 1 teaspoon crushed chillies in vinegar. Stir over low heat until heated through, then check the seasoning (some brands of soy beans are more salty than others). Sprinkle 2 teaspoons crushed fried peanuts over the sauce, then serve warm in a bowl alongside the steamed chicken breasts. The soy bean paste and chillies in vinegar are available from Asian speciality stores.

chilli and lime

IN a small bowl, combine 1–2 small fresh red chillies, seeds and membranes removed, and finely sliced, 2 crushed, small cloves of garlic, 1 teaspoon sugar, 3 tablespoons fish sauce and 2 tablespoons each of lime juice and water. Garnish with 2 teaspoons finely julienned carrot. Serve as a dipping sauce with the steamed chicken breasts.

miso

IN a small saucepan, heat 1/3 cup (80 ml) water, 1/2 teaspoon dashi powder, 1 teaspoon Japanese soy sauce and 1 tablespoon mirin. Whisk in 1 tablespoon white miso paste. Sprinkle with 2 teaspoons finely sliced spring onion. Serve in a bowl alongside the warm chicken breasts. The dashi powder, mirin and white miso paste are available from Asian speciality stores.

Marinated chicken

Marinating chicken before cooking with intense heat is an excellent way to make it juicy and delicious. The skin and bone add to the flavour.

1.2 kg chicken, trimmed of excess fat
  and cut into 10 pieces
1/3 cup (80 ml) olive oil
1 1/2 teaspoons chilli flakes
2 cloves garlic, chopped
pinch of saffron threads
1/2 cup (125 ml) lemon juice
1 cup (50 g) fresh mint

1 PUT the chicken pieces in a ceramic or glass bowl or dish. Ceramic and glass are ideal for marinating because metal reacts with acids such as lemon juice and plastic absorbs strong flavours. Use a dish that will hold the chicken in a single layer.

2 USING a blender or food processor, blend the remaining ingredients until well combined. Pour this mixture over the chicken, moving the pieces around to make sure they are well coated. Cover and refrigerate for 1 hour.

3 HEAT a chargrill plate or pan and add the chicken pieces, a few at a time. Cook until slightly charred, golden brown and cooked through. Keep each batch in a warm place while you cook the rest. Season with salt and pepper before serving with lemon wedges and extra mint.

4 WHEN chicken or other meat is marinated, a few things happen. Most marinades contain an acidic liquid, such as the lemon juice in this recipe, or another fruit juice, or wine, which helps to tenderise the flesh by breaking down the fibres. The marinade also permeates the flesh and adds flavour and moisture. Turn the page for more delicious marinade recipes.

SERVES 4.

MARINADES can be used for basting the chicken to help keep it moist during cooking and to add flavour. To do this, reserve 2 tablespoons of the marinade, before it goes on the raw chicken, then brush it on the chicken during cooking. To avoid contamination, don't use the residue of the marinade in which the chicken has marinated.

IF you don't have a chargrill plate or pan, barbecuing works just as well. Heat the barbecue before starting to cook so the intense heat will crisp the skin.

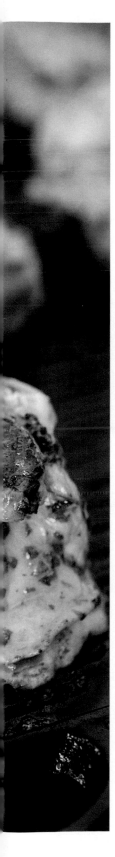

USING mint in the marinade gives a lovely, fresh flavour, but feel free to experiment. Basil, parsley, sage or a little rosemary are equally suitable.

IF you don't have a food processor, finely chop the marinade ingredients and mix together in a bowl. It will make little difference to the end result.

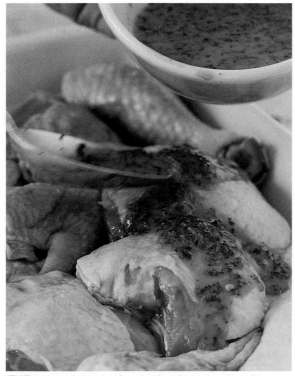

THE lemon juice in the marinade not only adds flavour to the dish, it also aids in tenderising the chicken pieces.

DISCARD the marinade after removing the chicken. Don't reuse it on raw or cooked chicken, otherwise contamination from salmonella may occur.

chicken marinades

five-spice

IN a glass or ceramic bowl, mix 2 teaspoons each of five-spice powder and kecap manis, 2 tablespoons each of dry sherry and soy sauce, and 1 tablespoon peanut oil. Set aside 2 teaspoons of the marinade for basting. Add four 200 g trimmed, skinless, boneless chicken breasts, stir to coat well, then cover and marinate in the refrigerator for at least 2 hours. Cook the chicken breasts on a hot chargrill for 6–8 minutes on both sides, basting with the reserved marinade occasionally, or until cooked through.

sweet chilli

IN a saucepan, combine $1/4$ cup (60 ml) water, $1/4$ cup (60 g) sugar, 2 tablespoons rice wine vinegar, 3 fresh red chillies, finely sliced, and 2 teaspoons grated fresh ginger. Simmer for 5 minutes, or until the sugar has dissolved and the mixture has thickened slightly. Remove from the heat, add 1 tablespoon peanut oil, $1/4$ cup (60 ml) kecap manis and $1/2$ teaspoon sesame oil. Stir, cool completely and put in a glass or ceramic dish. Set aside 2 teaspoons for basting. Add four 200 g trimmed, skinless, boneless chicken breasts to the dish and stir. Cover and chill for 2 hours. Cook on a hot chargrill for 6–8 minutes each side, basting with the reserved marinade, until cooked.

lemon, garlic and herb

IN a glass or ceramic bowl, combine $^1/_3$ cup (80 ml) lemon juice, $^1/_2$ teaspoon grated lemon rind, 3 crushed cloves garlic, 1 tablespoon olive oil, 2 tablespoons chopped fresh parsley and $^1/_2$ teaspoon chopped fresh rosemary. Set aside 2 teaspoons of the marinade for basting. Add four 200 g trimmed, skinless, boneless chicken breasts to the bowl, stir to coat well, then cover and marinate in the refrigerator for 2 hours. Cook the chicken on a hot chargrill for 6–8 minutes on both sides, basting with the reserved marinade occasionally, until cooked through.

coconut, lime and ginger

IN a glass or ceramic bowl, combine $^1/_3$ cup (80 ml) coconut milk, 2 tablespoons lime juice, $1^1/_2$ teaspoons grated fresh ginger, 1 finely sliced fresh kaffir lime leaf, 1 crushed clove garlic and 1 tablespoon vegetable oil. Set aside 2 teaspoons of marinade for basting. Add four 200 g trimmed, skinless, boneless chicken breasts to the bowl, stir to coat, then cover and marinate in the refrigerator for 2 hours. Cook the chicken on a hot chargrill for 6–8 minutes on both sides, basting with the reserved marinade occasionally, until cooked.

THE combination of dry spices gives tandoori its distinctive smoky flavour. Often, food colouring is added to give the familiar intense colour.

GHEE is clarified butter commonly used for cooking in India, especially in the north. Ghee withstands high temperatures, so it is good for frying.

YOGHURT is a key ingredient in Indian cooking. Apart from adding flavour, it also acts as a tenderiser, resulting in a delectably moist chicken.

Tandoori chicken

Traditionally, this dish is cooked in a 'tandoor', an unglazed earthen or clay oven shaped like a large jar, used throughout India and the Middle East.

CHARGRILLING or pan-frying allows the yoghurt marinade to form a wonderful smoky crust. However, you can also grill or roast the chicken.

1/2 teaspoon sweet smoked paprika
1 teaspoon paprika
1/2 teaspoon ground cumin
1/2 teaspoon ground coriander
1/4 teaspoon ground ginger
1/4 teaspoon ground cinnamon
1/4 teaspoon ground fenugreek seeds
1/4 teaspoon ground black pepper
1/4 teaspoon chilli powder
1/4 teaspoon ground cardamom
1/4 teaspoon ground caraway seeds
2 cloves garlic, crushed
2 tablespoons lemon juice
4 tablespoons finely chopped fresh coriander
1 cup (250 g) Greek-style or other thick natural yoghurt
6 boneless chicken breasts
20 g ghee

1 PREPARE the tandoori spice blend by mixing the sweet smoked paprika, paprika, cumin, coriander, ginger, cinnamon, fenugreek, black pepper, chilli powder, cardamom and caraway in a large ceramic or glass bowl or dish. Ceramic and glass are ideal for marinating because metal reacts with acids, such as lemon juice, and plastic absorbs strong flavours.

2 ADD the crushed garlic, lemon juice, fresh coriander and yoghurt to the bowl and stir the mixture together. Add the chicken breasts and coat thoroughly with the marinade. Cover and refrigerate for at least 8 hours, or overnight.

3 REMOVE the chicken from the marinade and lightly season each side with salt. Heat a chargrill pan or heavy-based frying pan. Add the ghee and when it is hot, but not smoking, add the chicken and cook over low heat for 8–10 minutes each side, or until cooked through.

SERVES 6.

SERVE the chicken with steamed basmati rice or rice pilaf, lemon wedges for squeezing, and some finely diced cucumber mixed with yoghurt.

Satay chicken

Satay sticks can be served as a first course, or a main with rice and a green salad. For a popular party piece, use smaller skewers with fewer chicken pieces.

500 g chicken thigh fillets, cut into 1 cm wide strips
1 clove garlic, crushed
2 teaspoons finely grated fresh ginger
3 teaspoons fish sauce

SATAY SAUCE
2 teaspoons peanut oil
4 red Asian shallots, finely chopped
4 cloves garlic, crushed
2 teaspoons finely chopped fresh ginger
2 fresh bird's eye chillies, seeded and finely chopped
1/2 cup (125 g) crunchy peanut butter
200 ml coconut milk
2 teaspoons soy sauce
2 tablespoons grated palm sugar
1 1/2 tablespoons fish sauce
1 fresh kaffir lime leaf
1 1/2 tablespoons lime juice

1 PUT the chicken, garlic, ginger and fish sauce in a glass or ceramic bowl and move the chicken around to coat well. Cover and refrigerate for 1 hour. Soak 12 wooden skewers in cold water for 30 minutes to prevent them burning during cooking.

2 MEANWHILE, to make the satay sauce, heat the oil in a saucepan over medium heat, then add the shallots, garlic, ginger and chilli. Stir constantly with a wooden spoon for 5 minutes, or until the shallots are golden. Reduce the heat to low and add the remaining sauce ingredients. Simmer for 10 minutes, or until thickened. Take off the heat and keep warm. Remove the kaffir lime leaf.

3 THREAD 2–3 chicken strips onto each skewer. Don't crowd the skewers or the chicken won't cook evenly. Cook the chicken on a heated barbecue or chargrill, turning the skewers after 5 minutes. Cook for another 5 minutes, or until they are cooked through. Serve with the sauce.

SERVES 4–6.

CHARGRILLING or barbecuing adds a fantastic smoky flavour to the chicken. However, cooking the satay sticks in a frying pan or under a grill also works well.

BIRD'S eye chillies, although small, are very hot. It's a good idea to wear rubber gloves when handling chillies, to prevent skin irritation.

LEFTOVER satay sauce will last for a week if stored, covered, in the refrigerator. Having it on hand means a delicious dish is only a few steps away.

WHEN threading the chicken onto the skewers, spread them out as you go and leave a small gap between each piece.

MAKE the grill or barbecue plate very hot and allow the underneath of the chicken to brown well before turning. If it sticks, it isn't ready to be turned.

COOK the chicken in batches so it doesn't stew in its juices, which will make it tough. Marinating the chicken before stir-frying gives a superior flavour.

TOSSING the ingredients during stir-frying ensures even cooking and prevents burning. The vegetables should retain their texture and firmness.

IT is important for the wok to be very hot as this will add that slightly smoky stir-fry flavour, known as "the breath of the wok", to the dish.

WHEN the cornflour is heated, it will thicken the sauce and give a glossy coating to the vegetables and chicken.

Chicken wrapped in prosciutto and sage

This delicious, simple dish makes the most of some quintessential Italian flavours. The sage permeates the chicken, while the prosciutto keeps the breast meat wonderfully moist.

4 chicken breast fillets
1 tablespoon lemon juice
1 tablespoon olive oil
2 cloves garlic, bruised and halved
3 large, fresh sage leaves, shredded
8 slices prosciutto
16 fresh sage leaves (preferably small to medium)
2 tablespoons olive oil

1 TRIM the chicken of excess fat and sinew and place in a glass or ceramic bowl or dish that will hold the chicken in a single layer. Don't use metal or plastic dishes. Mix the lemon juice, olive oil, garlic and shredded sage in a small bowl, add to the chicken and stir the chicken around to make sure it is coated all over with the marinade. Cover and refrigerate for 1 hour.

2 DISCARD the garlic and lightly season the chicken with salt and freshly ground black pepper. Wrap 2 slices of prosciutto around each breast fillet, tucking in 2 sage leaves on each side as you go. Make sure the leaves are secure, but not completely covered by the prosciutto. Secure the prosciutto with toothpicks. Using the heel of your hand, gently pound the breasts to flatten them slightly to ensure even cooking.

3 HEAT the oil in a heavy-based frying pan over medium–high heat and cook the breasts for 5 minutes each side, or until golden and cooked through. Leave the chicken to rest for a few minutes, then remove the toothpicks and serve. Delicious with soft polenta and a fresh green salad.

SERVES 4.

POLENTA is cornmeal, a speciality from Italy. It is cooked with water, milk or stock, and seasoning, and is served soft as shown here, or set in a tray, cut into pieces, then grilled.

sauces for pan-fried chicken

tarragon and mustard sauce

DRAIN the excess fat from the pan, add 20 g butter and gently cook 4 thinly sliced French eschallots over low heat until softened but not browned. Add $^{1}/_{2}$ cup (125 ml) dry white wine to the pan and cook over medium heat until nearly all the wine has evaporated. Add 1 cup (250 ml) each of white chicken stock (from page 14) and cream and simmer for 6–8 minutes, until the sauce has reduced and thickened. Stir in 2 tablespoons Dijon mustard and 1 tablespoon chopped fresh tarragon. Cook for another 2–3 minutes and season, to taste.

mushroom sauce

LEAVE the fat in the pan and add 20 g butter. When the butter begins to foam, add 350 g thinly sliced button mushrooms and cook over high heat for 5–6 minutes, tossing the pan constantly, and adding a little more butter, if necessary, until the mushrooms are lightly browned. Add 2 crushed cloves garlic and 2 teaspoons chopped fresh thyme and cook for another minute. Add $^{1}/_{3}$ cup (80 ml) dry white wine, cook until it has nearly all evaporated, then add $^{1}/_{2}$ cup (125 ml) brown chicken stock (from page 16) and $^{3}/_{4}$ cup (185 ml) cream. Bring to the boil, then reduce the heat and simmer for 5–6 minutes, or until the sauce has thickened and reduced. Season, to taste. (You can use field mushrooms instead of button mushrooms. Field mushrooms generally have more flavour but can turn the sauce a dark grey colour.)

sauces for pan-fried chicken

lemon and basil sauce

DRAIN the excess fat from the pan and add 100 g butter. Cook over medium heat until the butter turns light hazelnut, then add 2 tablespoons lemon juice and 4 tablespoons shredded fresh basil. Season lightly and serve immediately. Don't make this sauce ahead of time, otherwise the basil will turn brown. You can use parsley instead of basil if you wish. (To shred the basil without bruising it, you must use a very sharp knife. Layer a few leaves on top of one another, roll up lengthways into a tight roll and shred the basil.)

marsala sauce

TIP the excess fat from the pan, add $^1/_2$ cup (125 ml) dry Marsala and cook over medium heat for 1–2 minutes, using a wooden spoon to scrape the brownings off the base of the pan. Add $^1/_2$ cup (125 ml) brown chicken stock (from page 16) and $^1/_3$ cup (80 ml) cream. Bring to the boil, then reduce the heat and simmer for 5–6 minutes, or until thickened and reduced. Strain the sauce to remove any sediment.

chicken breast stuffed with bocconcini, tomato and basil

USING a sharp knife, make a long slit horizontally through the length of 4 chicken breasts, being careful not to cut all the way through. Stuff each of these pockets with 2 fresh basil leaves, 60 g thinly sliced bocconcini and 2 pieces of semi-dried tomato. Fold each fillet over and secure with toothpicks. Cook as for the chicken breasts, but allow an extra 1–2 minutes on each side. Deglaze the pan with $^1/_4$ cup (60 ml) dry white wine. Stir in 1 teaspoon grated lemon rind, then drizzle this sauce over the hot chicken.

RESTING the chicken breast after cooking allows the flesh to 'relax', which helps retain the moisture in the flesh and makes it very succulent to eat.

The perfect pan-fried chicken breast

This quick, easy method of cooking is suitable for small portions of chicken. Boneless chicken breasts are ideal for pocketing and stuffing with filling.

4 skinless chicken breast fillets, tenderloins removed
30 g butter
1½ tablespoons oil

1 TRIM the breasts of any excess fat and sinew, then place them flat on a work surface. Lay the side of a large knife on the fattest part of one of the breasts. Push down gently but firmly with your fist to make the breast a more even thickness. Repeat with each breast. Season them all lightly with sea salt and freshly ground black pepper.

2 HEAT a heavy-based frying pan over medium–high heat, add the butter and oil, and when it is hot but not burning, add the breasts and cook for about 5 minutes each side, or until golden and cooked through (this may take an extra 1–2 minutes each side, depending on the size of the breasts). The meat is done when just springy to the touch. Transfer to warm plates and leave to rest for 2 minutes, or while making a sauce, before serving. Turn the page for some delicious sauce recipes.

SERVES 4.

INCLUDING the wing bone helps keep a plump shape and the skin provides extra flavour. However, as breasts are usually sold skinless and boneless, you will probably have to buy a whole chicken and cut off the breasts yourself. You could also try talking to your chicken supplier.

IF you are removing the breast fillets from a whole chicken, pull off the white tenderloins that are on the underside because they tend to draw the meat out of shape during cooking. Cut 1 cm along two sides of its exposed end, hold the end with a tea towel and pull the tenderloin out, scraping it free against your knife. These can be frozen, along with the remaining Marylands. The carcass and wing tips can be used to make a stock.

FLATTENING the breasts means they cook evenly throughout. Boneless chicken thigh pieces can also be pan-fried.

THE butter adds more flavour to the dish than just oil would provide, but you need to use a combination of both to stop the butter burning too easily.

Stir-fried chicken with chilli caramel sauce

1/2 teaspoon five-spice powder

2 tablespoons grated fresh ginger

2 tablespoons soy sauce

1/4 cup (60 ml) Chinese rice wine or dry sherry

4 cloves garlic, crushed

800 g chicken thigh fillets, cubed

1/3 cup (45 g) soft brown sugar

1/4 cup (60 ml) rice vinegar

2 tablespoons sweet chilli sauce

2 tablespoons fish sauce

1/4 cup (60 ml) white chicken stock from page 14

1/4 cup (60 ml) peanut oil

1 small fresh red chilli, seeded and finely chopped

3 tablespoons fresh coriander, finely chopped

4 spring onions, thinly sliced on the diagonal, to garnish

1 PUT the five-spice, ginger, soy sauce, wine and half the garlic in a glass or ceramic bowl, add 1 teaspoon salt and 1/2 teaspoon ground black pepper, then stir together. Add the chicken, stir to coat, then cover and marinate in the refrigerator for at least 4 hours. Glass and ceramic are ideal for marinating because metal reacts with acids and plastic absorbs strong flavours.

2 IN a small bowl or jug, combine the brown sugar, rice vinegar, sweet chilli sauce, fish sauce and chicken stock.

3 HEAT the wok and add 2 tablespoons oil. When the oil starts to smoke, add the chicken in batches and stir-fry for about 3–4 minutes, until golden brown. Remove each batch and keep warm while you cook the rest.

4 REDUCE the heat slightly and heat the remaining oil in the wok. Add the chilli and remaining garlic, and cook for 30 seconds. Pour in the sauce mixture and allow it to bubble until reduced, syrupy and caramelised. This will take about 3–5 minutes. When the sauce is thoroughly reduced and caramelised, return the chicken to the wok, without any of the accumulated juices, and cook for 1 minute to coat the chicken in the sauce and heat through. Stir in the coriander. Garnish with the spring onion before serving.

SERVES 4.

THIS is a rich, sweet and spicy stir-fry that is delicious with steamed jasmine rice. Serve with separate dishes of vegetables, such as bok choy, steamed with ginger.

MOVE the chicken around constantly in the wok to ensure even cooking. When cooking in batches, let the wok reheat after removing each batch.

RICE vinegar is a mild vinegar and features in Japanese and south-east Asian cooking. For example, it is used in sushi rice.

AS it reduces, the brown sugar caramelises, making the sauce syrupy and sticky. The vinegar perfectly balances the sweetness.

IF you prefer your sauce to glaze and coat the chicken, remove the hot chicken and boil the sauce until reduced to your preferred consistency.

STIR-FRY the chicken in batches so you don't overcrowd the wok. If you cook too much at once, it will stew in the juices and become tough.

HOKKIEN noodles are thick, fresh egg noodles. They have been cooked and lightly oiled before being packaged.

SUCCESSFUL stir-frying depends on heating the wok until it's very hot and making sure you toss the ingredients constantly to evenly distribute the heat.

THIS curry is mildly spiced but if you would like a little more heat, add 1 small, seeded and finely chopped fresh red chilli.

MARINATED STIR-FRIED CHICKEN WITH COCONUT CURRY SAUCE 49

DON'T marinate in metal dishes because they will react with acids such as lemon juice. Plastic dishes absorb strong flavours, so glass or ceramic is best.

FRESH sage leaves are grey-green, soft and velvety, with a subtle but pervasive flavour. Don't use dried sage as it is too strong for this dish.

PROSCIUTTO is Italian cured ham. Originally from the Parma region, the ham is salted and hung for up to 2 years. It is very thinly sliced for use.

THE cooking time will vary according to the thickness of the chicken breasts. Test with a skewer. When the chicken is ready, the juices will run clear.

CHICKEN WRAPPED IN PROSCIUTTO AND SAGE   57

WHEN pounding chicken with a mallet, plastic wrap protects the flesh and makes it easier for you to flatten out the flesh for more even cooking.

FLOURING the chicken is important to ensure that the egg coats the surface evenly so that the breadcrumbs will stick.

MAKE sure you allow excess egg to drip off before coating with breadcrumbs, otherwise the crumb will be gluggy, and may fall off when pan-fried.

FOR a different flavour, add some grated lemon rind and chopped parsley or other fresh herbs to the fresh breadcrumbs.

Chicken schnitzel

This method of coating the fillets before frying makes the basis for a delicious lunch or dinner. It can also be used for making veal schnitzel.

4 skinless chicken breast fillets, tenderloins removed
1/4 cup (30 g) plain flour
2 cups (160 g) fresh white breadcrumbs
1 large egg
2 tablespoons milk
60 g butter
3 tablespoons vegetable oil

1 PLACE the chicken fillets between sheets of plastic wrap, then, using a meat mallet or rolling pin, gently flatten each fillet to a thickness of about 1 cm.

2 PUT the flour on a plate and season with salt and pepper. Put the breadcrumbs on another plate. Beat the egg and the milk together in a shallow bowl.

3 COAT each breast firstly in the seasoned flour, then dip in the egg and finally the breadcrumbs, making sure each breast is completely covered. Refrigerate the fillets for 30 minutes.

4 MELT half the butter and half the oil together in a frying pan. Cook the fillets, in batches if necessary, making sure they are well separated in the pan. Keep the heat at moderate so that the butter sizzles but doesn't smoke. After 5 minutes, turn the schnitzels with tongs to ensure an even crust. They should be cooked through after another 5 minutes. Use the remaining oil and butter, if necessary, during frying and after each batch. Drain on paper towels and serve with lemon wedges.

SERVES 4.

IF you would like a crisper crust, use a combination of half dried breadcrumbs and half cornflake crumbs.

FOR a lighter alternative, use dried breadcrumbs for the coating, brush or spray with oil and bake in a moderately hot (190°C/375°F/Gas 5) oven for 20–25 minutes.

FOR a schnitzel Milanese, top the schnitzels with fresh tomato sauce and grated mozzarella, then gently grill under a medium grill until lightly browned.

Chicken breast with garlic and balsamic vinegar

This delicious version of sautéed chicken has a wonderfully piquant sauce made with rich brown stock, balsamic vinegar, lemon juice and garlic.

4 chicken breasts, skin on, tenderloins removed
20 g butter
1 tablespoon olive oil
12 whole cloves garlic, skin on, ends cut off
1/3 cup (80 ml) balsamic vinegar
1/4 cup (60 ml) brown chicken stock from page 16
1 tablespoon lemon juice
2 tablespoons chopped fresh parsley
1 teaspoon fresh thyme leaves

1 TRIM the chicken of any sinew and excess fat. In a heavy-based frying pan, heat the butter and olive oil. Add the garlic cloves and sauté until golden all over.

2 LIGHTLY season the chicken breasts on both sides, then put them skin-side-down in the pan and cook for 5 minutes, or until golden brown. Turn them over and cook for 5 minutes, or until just cooked through. They should feel springy to the touch. Leave them in the pan.

3 ADD the balsamic vinegar, chicken stock, lemon juice and herbs to the pan. Bring to the boil, then reduce the heat and simmer for 2–3 minutes, until reduced and slightly syrupy. Season well with sea salt and freshly ground black pepper. Serve the chicken immediately with the whole garlic cloves and the sauce.

SERVES 4.

DON'T be worried about the number of garlic cloves in this recipe because the flesh softens and the flavour mellows considerably as the garlic cooks.

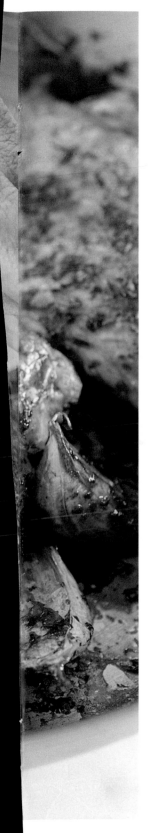

TRIMMING the very top end of the garlic before cooking makes it easier to squeeze the softened garlic flesh over the chicken before eating.

LEMON juice adds flavour and contains acid, which helps to tenderise the chicken by breaking down the fibres.

FRESH herbs retain more of their flavour if you chop them not long before you are going to use them. Grow your own so that they are always on hand.

BALSAMIC vinegar is made from boiled-down must, which is the concentrated sweet juice of white grapes.

DON'T be afraid to use your fingers to rub the mustard and tarragon mixture well into the chicken flesh.

ALLOWING the chicken skin to become golden and caramelised at this stage adds flavour and colour to the finished dish.

USE the back of the spoon to incorporate the flour as well as you can into the pan drippings. This helps avoid lumps in the sauce.

TO make sure the sauce is lump-free, beat it well with a balloon whisk before pouring evenly over the chicken.

TRY adding a few orange sweet potatoes to the mash.
Steam until tender, then mash with butter and seasoning.
Add cream until you have the desired consistency.

Creamy chicken with tarragon and mustard

Tarragon has a strong, unique flavour which goes very well with chicken. In this recipe it is mixed with the mustard and left on the chicken overnight.

1.5 kg chicken, cut into 8 pieces
2½ tablespoons wholegrain mustard
1 teaspoon chopped fresh tarragon, plus extra to garnish
45 g butter
2 teaspoons olive oil
85 g streaky bacon or mild pancetta, finely chopped
3 French eschallots, finely chopped
2 cloves garlic, finely chopped
1 tablespoon plain flour
3/4 cup (185 ml) dry white wine
1¼ cups (315 ml) white chicken stock from page 14
1/2 cup (125 ml) cream

1 PREHEAT the oven to moderate (180°C/350°F/Gas 4). Put the chicken pieces in a glass or ceramic dish. Mix 1½ tablespoons mustard with the chopped tarragon and rub the mixture all over the chicken pieces. Cover and refrigerate overnight.

2 MELT the butter and oil in a frying pan over medium–high heat and brown the chicken joints in two batches until the skin is golden. Transfer to a lidded ovenproof casserole.

3 ADD the bacon, eschallots and garlic to the pan and cook until the bacon just starts to brown. Stir in the flour and cook for 1 minute. Add the wine, stock and remaining mustard and cook for about 5 minutes, until the sauce is smooth. Pour over the chicken, then cover and bake for 1 hour 10 minutes.

4 REMOVE the chicken from the pan. Stir the cream into the sauce, then reduce the sauce over high heat until it reaches a coating consistency.

5 ADD the chicken to the sauce and stir until well coated. Serve on a platter with the sauce poured over the chicken. Garnish with the extra tarragon. Serve with mashed potato and green vegetables or salad.

SERVES 4.

Chicken cacciatora

This classic dish, originally from central Italy, has travelled widely and evolved along the way into many versions, each with its own subtle touch.

1 kg ripe tomatoes, preferably vine-ripened,
   or 2 x 425 g cans good-quality crushed tomatoes
1.5 kg chicken, cut into 8 pieces
2 tablespoons olive oil
2 onions, sliced
2 cloves garlic, finely chopped
2 tablespoons tomato paste
1 teaspoon sugar
1$^1/_2$ tablespoons finely chopped fresh rosemary
2 bay leaves
$^3/_4$ cup (185 ml) dry white wine
$^1/_2$ cup (125 ml) white chicken stock from page 14
1 tablespoon lemon juice
$^1/_2$ cup (80 g) kalamata olives (optional)

1 IF you are using fresh tomatoes, peel and seed them and cut into smallish dice.

2 CUT any excess skin and fat from the chicken pieces, and season them well with salt and black pepper. Heat the oil in a heavy-based frying pan over medium–high heat and cook the chicken pieces a few at a time until golden brown. Remove from the pan.

3 ADD the onion to the pan and cook over low heat until wilted and just starting to caramelise (this will take about 10 minutes). Don't let it brown too much. Add the tomato, garlic, tomato paste, sugar, herbs, wine and stock, bring to the boil, then reduce the heat and simmer, uncovered, for 15 minutes, or until reduced by about half.

4 ADD the chicken pieces to the sauce and season well with salt and pepper. Add the lemon juice, cover and cook over very low heat for 30 minutes. Add the olives, then remove from the heat and leave, covered, for 10 minutes.

5 SERVE the cacciatora with buttered noodles or a green salad.

SERVES 4.

"CACCIATORA" means "hunter" and is simple Italian peasant food. Some versions include sliced mushrooms, which should be sautéed with the onion.

Marinated stir-fried chicken with coconut curry sauce

400 g chicken breast fillets, trimmed of all fat and sinew
1 tablespoon dry sherry
1½ tablespoons soy sauce
½ cup (125 ml) coconut cream
½ cup (125 ml) white chicken stock from page 14
1½ teaspoons curry powder (mild madras)
¼ teaspoon sugar
450 g hokkien noodles
1 teaspoon sesame oil
2 tablespoons oil
1 onion, sliced
2 cloves garlic, crushed
1 tablespoon grated fresh ginger
200 g snow peas, cut on the diagonal

1 CUT the chicken breasts across the grain into 1.5 cm slices and put them in a glass or ceramic bowl (don't use metal or plastic). Add the sherry and 1 tablespoon soy sauce, stir until the chicken is well coated, then cover and refrigerate for 30 minutes.

2 IN a separate bowl, mix the coconut cream, chicken stock, curry powder, sugar and remaining soy sauce.

3 PUT the noodles in a large bowl, cover with boiling water and leave them for 1 minute to soften. Drain well, then separate the noodles and toss them with the sesame oil.

4 DRAIN the chicken pieces. Heat 1 tablespoon oil in a wok and when it is smoking, add half the chicken and stir-fry it for 2–3 minutes, until cooked through. Transfer to a bowl. Repeat with the remaining chicken then add, with any liquid, to the bowl. Return the wok to the heat, add the remaining oil and, when it is hot, add the onion and stir-fry for 1 minute. Add the garlic and ginger, cook for a few seconds, then return the chicken to the wok with the snow peas. Stir in the sauce mixture, as well as any liquid from the chicken.

5 ADD the noodles to the wok and toss until everything is heated through. Serve immediately.

SERVES 4.

GREEN beans or snake beans, diagonally cut into short lengths, are a great alternative to snow peas. Garnish the stir-fry with coriander and shredded spring onion, if desired.

lime, chilli and basil

IN a small bowl, combine $1/4$ cup (60 ml) lime juice, 1–2 small fresh red chillies, finely chopped with the seeds left in, $1^1/2$ tablespoons fish sauce, 1 teaspoon shaved palm sugar and 1 teaspoon cornflour. Mix well, then add to the wok instead of the sauce on page 45. Toss in the wok for 3 minutes, or until the mixture has thickened slightly to coat all the ingredients. Remove from the heat, add 4 tablespoons fresh basil and quickly stir through.

plum and ginger

IN a small bowl, combine $1/2$ cup (125 ml) Chinese plum sauce, 2 teaspoons grated fresh ginger, $1/4$ cup (60 ml) white chicken stock from page 14, 2 teaspoons rice vinegar and $1/4$ teaspoon cornflour. Mix well, then add to the wok instead of the sauce on page 45. Toss in the wok for 3 minutes, or until the mixture has thickened slightly to coat all the ingredients. Remove from the heat, then add the coriander and spring onion and quickly stir through.

stir-fry sauces

blackbean

DRAIN and rinse 3 tablespoons of canned, salted blackbeans in a strainer. Combine in a small bowl with 2 tablespoons white chicken stock from page 14, 1 teaspoon each of cornflour, sugar and sesame oil, and 3 tablespoons blackbean sauce. Mix well with a fork, crushing the blackbeans. Add to the wok instead of the sauce on page 45. Bring to the boil, then toss in the wok for 3 minutes, or until the mixture has thickened slightly to coat the ingredients. Remove from the heat, then add the coriander and spring onion and quickly toss through. Check the seasoning and adjust if necessary.

sesame, soy and honey

IN a small bowl, combine 3 teaspoons honey, 1½ teaspoons sesame oil, 2 tablespoons toasted sesame seeds, 1 teaspoon cornflour and ¼ cup (60 ml) each of soy sauce and white chicken stock, from page 14. Mix well, then add to the wok instead of the sauce on page 45. Toss in the wok for 3 minutes, or until the mixture has thickened slightly to coat all the ingredients. Remove from the heat, then add the coriander and spring onion and quickly toss through.

STIR-FRYING is a fast cooking method so it is wise to have all your ingredients measured and chopped before you begin. Alternative stir-fry sauces are shown on the next page.

Chicken and vegetable stir-fry

1 tablespoon light soy sauce
2 cloves garlic, crushed
1 teaspoon grated fresh ginger
1½ teaspoons sesame oil
600 g chicken thigh fillets, cut in half lengthways,
   then across the grain into 6 pieces
2 tablespoons peanut oil
1 onion, cut into 16 wedges
150 g snow peas, topped, tailed, string removed,
   cut in half on the diagonal
250 g bok choy
115 g baby corn, sliced in half on the diagonal
4 tablespoons chopped fresh coriander
2 spring onions, finely sliced on the diagonal

STIR-FRY SAUCE
¼ cup (60 ml) oyster sauce
¼ cup (60 ml) white chicken stock from page 14
2 teaspoons soy sauce
1 teaspoon cornflour

1 IN a glass or ceramic bowl, mix the light soy sauce, garlic, ginger and ½ teaspoon sesame oil. Add the chicken and stir to coat well. Cover and marinate in the refrigerator for 2 hours. Glass and ceramic are ideal for marinating because metal reacts with acids and plastic absorbs strong flavours.

2 MIX all the stir-fry sauce ingredients in a small bowl until the cornflour is thoroughly incorporated.

3 HEAT a wok over high heat and add 1 tablespoon peanut oil and the remaining sesame oil. When hot, add the chicken in batches and stir-fry until just cooked through. Add a little more oil if required. Remove from the wok.

4 HEAT the remaining peanut oil in the wok. Add the onion, stir-fry for 2–3 minutes, then add the snow peas, bok choy and baby corn and stir-fry for 3 minutes. Add the stir-fry sauce and the chicken with any juices. Stir well and cook for about 3 minutes, until the sauce has thickened to lightly coat the chicken and vegetables. Remove from the heat, and stir in the coriander and spring onion. Season and serve with rice. Turn the page for more delicious stir-fry sauces.

SERVES 4.

BE careful not to overcrowd the pan when browning the chicken. If you do, the pan will lose heat and the chicken will stew instead of colour.

VINE-RIPENED tomatoes come to full maturity on the vine and have a deeper, sweeter flavour, which adds to the richness of the sauce.

TO peel tomatoes, score the ends with a sharp knife and plunge into boiling water for 10 seconds. Refresh in cold water, then peel and seed.

WHILE the chicken is cooking in the sauce, check occasionally to ensure that it has not caught on the bottom of the pan.

MAKE sure the chicken pieces are only cooked at a gentle simmer. Boiling will result in toughened, dry meat.

COOKING the mushrooms separately before adding them to the sauce gives them more flavour and helps make a richer dish.

STRAIN the stock to remove the vegetables and any chicken remnants. Wipe out the pan before returning the stock to ensure a smooth sauce.

AN alternative to this cornflour thickener is a mixture of equal parts flour and room-temperature butter, slowly whisked into the simmering stock.

Chicken fricassee

Traditionally, the chicken in a fricassee should be sealed without browning or cooked directly in the liquid to retain the dish's distinctive pale colour.

1.8–2 kg chicken, cut into 8 pieces
1.25 litres white chicken stock from page 14
2 onions, roughly chopped
2 celery sticks, roughly chopped
1 bay leaf
20 g butter
150 g baby button mushrooms, sliced
2 egg yolks
2 teaspoons cornflour
$1/3$ cup (80 ml) cream
2 tablespoons finely chopped fresh parsley

1 PUT the chicken in a large saucepan, add the chicken stock, onion, celery and bay leaf and bring slowly to the boil, skimming off any scum that appears on the surface. Reduce the heat to low, cover and simmer for 30 minutes.

2 WHILE the chicken is cooking, heat the butter in a small frying pan until foaming, add the mushrooms and cook for a few minutes until cooked through. Drain on paper towels.

3 REMOVE the chicken from the stock with a slotted spoon and keep it warm. Strain the stock and wipe the pan clean. Return the stock to the pan and, over moderate to high heat, reduce the stock by half. In a small bowl, mix the egg yolks, cornflour and cream. Slowly whisk the egg mixture into the stock. Don't let the mixture boil, just let it heat through and thicken. Season with salt and white pepper.

4 ADD the chicken and mushrooms to the sauce and gently stir to coat. Place 2 portions of chicken on each plate and sprinkle with the parsley.

SERVES 4.

AS a variation, when you return the mushrooms and chicken to the pan, add a drained 200 g can of marinated, cooked artichoke hearts.

DIFFERENT types of mushrooms, such as Swiss brown, field or pine mushrooms can be used instead of (or as well as) the button mushrooms.

Coq au vin

The characteristic flavour of this French casserole comes from the red wine in which the chicken is marinated overnight.

1.5 kg chicken, cut into 8 pieces
2 cups (500 ml) good-quality red
    wine
a bouquet garni (including thyme,
    bay leaf and parsley)
1 tablespoon olive oil
125 g speck, skin discarded, cut
    into 2 cm x 1 cm pieces
1 onion, chopped
2 cloves garlic, crushed

25 ml brandy
1 tablespoon plain flour
1 tablespoon tomato paste
2 cups (500 ml) white chicken
    stock from page 14
12 baby onions, peeled
60 g unsalted butter, chilled
12 button mushrooms
chopped fresh parsley, for serving

1 PLACE the chicken pieces in a glass or ceramic dish and add the red wine and bouquet garni. Cover and marinate in the refrigerator overnight.

2 IN a heavy, cast-iron pan, heat the oil over medium–high heat and add the speck. Cook until it renders some of its fat and is golden brown. Drain on paper towels, leaving the fat in the pan.

3 PAT the chicken dry and retain the marinade and bouquet garni. Fry the chicken pieces 3 or 4 at a time until they start to change colour. Remove from the pan. Add the onion and cook for 1 minute. Add the garlic and brandy and cook until all the liquid has evaporated. Stir in the flour and the tomato paste. Deglaze the pan with the reserved marinade and bouquet garni and reduce the liquid by half. Return the chicken to the pan, then add enough stock to cover the chicken pieces. Bring to the boil, cover then reduce the heat and simmer for 30 minutes.

4 WHILE the chicken is cooking, bring a saucepan of salted water to the boil and blanch the baby onions for 8 minutes. Drain them and discard the water. In the same pan, melt 20 g of the butter, add the button mushrooms and cook for 4 minutes, then remove from the pan.

5 WHEN the chicken has been cooking for 30 minutes, add the mushrooms and baby onions to the pan and cook for another 10 minutes.

6 USING a slotted spoon, transfer the chicken and vegetables to a platter. Remove the bouquet garni. Return the pan to the heat and boil vigorously to reduce by almost half. Cut the remaining butter into small cubes and whisk it one piece at a time into the sauce until the sauce is rich and glossy. Strain the sauce over the chicken and sprinkle with the parsley.

SERVES 4.

TRADITIONALLY, an older cock or hen was used, so a long marinating time was essential to tenderise the bird.

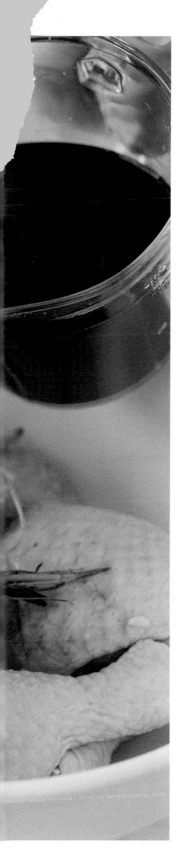

DON'T overcrowd the pan when frying the chicken, otherwise the chicken will not cook quickly enough and instead will stew in its juices and toughen.

DEGLAZING means to add liquid to the pan to dissolve caramelised juices stuck to the bottom of the pan.

REDUCING the sauce thickens it and whisking in small portions of butter turns it into a richer, glossier coating for the chicken.

ALL this dish needs to complement it is a handful of boiled new potatoes and a fresh green salad.

IF you like your food very spicy, add an extra 1/4 teaspoon cayenne pepper to the spice mix before coating the chicken.

CHORIZO is a cured sausage made from minced or chopped pork that has as its flavourings black pepper, garlic and paprika or the pulp from red capsicum.

THE rendered fat from the chorizo and chicken enhances the rich flavour of this dish.

DON'T be tempted to stir the mixture in the pan after you have added the liquid, or the rice will become gluggy.

Chicken jambalaya

This Creole or Cajun dish appears to have French origins. It is a spicy stew, usually with rice, chicken, prawns and vegetables.

1 teaspoon paprika
3/4 teaspoon dried basil
3/4 teaspoon dried thyme
1/2 teaspoon ground white pepper
1/2 teaspoon ground black pepper
1/4 teaspoon cayenne pepper
1/2 teaspoon dried oregano
3/4 teaspoon garlic powder
3/4 teaspoon onion powder
500 g chicken thigh fillets, each
    cut into 4 pieces
2 tablespoons vegetable oil
250 g chorizo, cut into 1 cm slices
1 large onion, chopped
2 celery sticks, sliced

1 large green capsicum, cut into
    rough 2 cm pieces
4 cloves garlic, crushed
2 teaspoons fresh thyme
400 g can chopped tomatoes
2 bay leaves
1/4 teaspoon Tabasco
1 cup (200 g) long-grain white rice
3 1/2 cups (875 ml) hot white
    chicken stock from page 14
450 g raw prawns (optional),
    peeled, tails intact
5 spring onions, finely sliced
3 tablespoons chopped fresh
    parsley

1 PLACE the paprika, basil, thyme, white pepper, black pepper, cayenne, oregano, garlic powder, onion powder and 3/4 teaspoon salt in a bowl. Add the chicken thigh pieces and mix to coat the chicken well.

2 HEAT the vegetable oil in a wide, heavy-based frying pan over medium heat and cook the chorizo for 5–6 minutes, or until lightly browned. Remove with a slotted spoon, leaving as much oil in the pan as possible. Add the chicken to the pan in batches and cook over medium heat for 6–8 minutes, until lightly browned, adding a little more oil if necessary. Remove from the pan with a slotted spoon, leaving as much fat in the pan as possible.

3 ADD the onion, celery, capsicum, garlic and thyme to the pan and cook over medium heat for 6–8 minutes, stirring often with a wooden spoon to lift the scrapings from the base of the pan. When the vegetables begin to brown, add the tomato, bay leaves and Tabasco and simmer for 2–3 minutes.

4 RETURN the chorizo and chicken to the pan. Add the rice, stir briefly and add the stock. Don't stir at this point. Reduce the heat and simmer, uncovered, for 25–30 minutes, or until all the liquid has been absorbed and the rice is tender. Remove from the heat and add the prawns, if using them. Cover and leave for 10 minutes, then fluff the rice with a fork, season well and stir in the spring onion and parsley.

SERVES 4–6.

AFTER fluffing the rice, serve the jambalaya straight from the pan at the table with a simple green salad.

Spicy chicken curry

Curry powders are believed to have originated in India. Make your own so you can experiment and use more of the spices you prefer.

CURRY POWDER
(makes 4 tablespoons)
2 teaspoons cumin seeds
2 teaspoons coriander seeds
2 teaspoons fenugreek seeds
1 teaspoon yellow mustard seeds
1 teaspoon black peppercorns
2 whole cloves
1 teaspoon chilli powder
2 teaspoons ground turmeric
1/2 teaspoon ground cinnamon
1/2 teaspoon ground cardamom
1 teaspoon ground ginger

1 tablespoon oil
1 large onion, finely chopped
2 cloves garlic, crushed
1 teaspoon grated fresh ginger
800 g chicken thigh fillets, cut
   into quarters
1 tablespoon tomato paste
2 teaspoons lemon juice
200 g ripe tomatoes, peeled
   and finely chopped
1 cup (250 ml) white chicken stock
   from page 14
1/2 cup (125 ml) coconut milk
4 curry leaves
1/2 cup (15 g) fresh coriander,
   finely chopped

SPICES are often dry-roasted to give more depth to the flavour. Remove them from the heat as soon as they are aromatic.

1 FOR the curry powder, heat a small frying pan over low heat, add the cumin, coriander, fenugreek and yellow mustard seeds, peppercorns and cloves. Shake the pan over the heat for 1–2 minutes, or until the spices are aromatic. Transfer to a spice grinder or mortar and pestle and grind to a fine powder. Mix in a small bowl with the remaining spices.

2 HEAT a heavy-based saucepan over low heat, add 2 tablespoons of the curry powder and dry-fry for 20 seconds, stirring constantly with a wooden spoon, being careful not to burn the spices. Stir in the oil to make a paste. Add the onion, garlic and ginger and stir for 2 minutes.

3 ADD the chicken pieces to the pan and cook until they are golden and coated all over with the spices. Add the tomato paste and cook for another 3 minutes. Stir in the lemon juice, chopped peeled tomatoes, chicken stock, coconut milk and curry leaves, bring to the boil, then reduce the heat to low and simmer for 1 hour, or until the chicken is very tender and the sauce reduced. Stir in the chopped coriander. Season well with salt and serve with steamed basmati rice.

SERVES 4.

CURRY leaves impart a wonderful fragrance, especially when fresh. They are available fresh and dried from Asian food stores.

KEEP the leftover curry powder in an airtight container for future use. Buy small quantities of spices to ensure freshness.

STIR the curry occasionally to make sure that it does not catch and burn on the bottom of the pan.

CURRY powder, a mix of hot and sweet spices, ground into a powder, is used in this dish to transform a basic stew into an aromatic delight. The proportions of the spices can be varied according to your taste.

SPICES such as cumin and coriander come in either seed or powder form. The seeds can generally be stored for a longer time than ground spices.

IN many Moroccan dishes, a mixture of spices is often toasted lightly in a dry pan before being ground and rubbed over the food to be cooked.

COOK the chicken over medium heat so the spices do not burn. Don't worry if the chicken is not cooked all the way through at this point.

HARISSA is a fiery mixture made from chillies and spices used often in Moroccan cooking. Sambal oelek can be used as a substitute.

COUSCOUS is a light grain product, which is a staple throughout North Africa and in Morocco. Instant couscous is readily available and easy to prepare.

Chicken tagine

Tagine means 'stew' and is a traditional Moroccan style of slow cooking. It shares its name with the vessel in which it is cooked — an earthenware dish with a distinctive pointed cover.

1 teaspoon cumin seeds
1 teaspoon coriander seeds
1 teaspoon ground ginger
1 teaspoon ground turmeric
1 teaspoon ground cinnamon
pinch of saffron threads
1/2 teaspoon dried chilli flakes
1 kg chicken thigh fillets, cut into halves
2 tablespoons olive oil
2 brown onions, chopped
4 cloves garlic, crushed
2 cups (500 ml) white chicken stock from page 14
2 large tomatoes, peeled, seeded and roughly chopped
1/4 cup (70 g) fresh dates, pitted and quartered
1/3 cup (85 g) sun-dried apricots (if big, cut in half)
1/2 cup (80 g) blanched almonds, toasted
chopped fresh coriander, to garnish

1 HEAT a large frying pan over low heat and add the cumin and coriander seeds, ginger, turmeric, cinnamon, saffron and chilli flakes. Shake the pan over the heat for 1–2 minutes, or until the spices are aromatic, then transfer to a mortar and pestle or spice grinder, and grind to a fine powder.

2 REMOVE all the fat and sinew from the chicken. Sprinkle with the dry spice mixture, retaining any that is left. Heat the oil in the frying pan over medium heat and cook the chicken pieces on both sides until lightly golden. Drain well on paper towels.

3 IN the same pan, cook the onion over medium heat for 5 minutes, or until golden. Add the garlic, stock, tomato and remaining spice mixture. Add the chicken, bring to the boil, then cover, reduce the heat and simmer for 25 minutes. Add the dates and apricots and cook for 25 minutes, or until the mixture thickens slightly. Season, then stir in the nuts. Garnish with the coriander, and serve with steamed couscous. Traditionally served with harissa on the side.

SERVES 4.

WARM naan bread is a perfect accompaniment to this comforting dish. Naan bread is becoming increasingly available from supermarkets, or just pick some up from your local Indian restaurant.

TOASTING spices modifies the flavour, resulting in more depth. Remove from the pan so that they don't continue toasting.

GARAM masala translates as 'hot mixture' and is a staple spice blend in most Indian households.

WHEN browning the chicken let it colour on one side before stirring. Frequent stirring causes heat loss.

SCRAPE up any sediment while you pour in the liquid ingredients so that it doesn't catch and burn.

Indian butter chicken

This dish is available at all the roadside eating houses of northwest India and is now popular all over the world.

2 tablespoons tandoori spice blend
   from page 41
100 g butter
1 tablespoon canola oil
800 g chicken thigh fillets, trimmed
   of all fat and sinew, each cut into
   chunks
1 onion, finely diced
2 large cloves garlic, crushed
1 teaspoon ground cumin
1 teaspoon paprika
1½ teaspoons garam masala

2 tablespoons tomato paste
1 cup (250 ml) white chicken stock
   from page 14
1 cup (250 ml) thick cream
1 teaspoon sugar
1 tablespoon ground almonds
⅓ cup (80 g) natural yoghurt
3 tablespoons finely chopped
   fresh coriander

1 HEAT a large, heavy-based saucepan over low heat, add the tandoori spice blend and dry-fry, shaking the pan occasionally, for 1–2 minutes, or until fragrant. Be careful the spices don't burn. Transfer to a small bowl.

2 MELT 20 g of the butter with the canola oil in the saucepan over medium heat. Add the chicken in batches and cook until golden. Remove from the pan.

3 MELT the remaining butter in the same pan. Add the onion, garlic, cumin, paprika and garam masala and cook for 2 minutes, or until fragrant. Add the tandoori spice blend and tomato paste and cook for another 2 minutes. Add the chicken stock, cream and sugar, then reduce the heat and simmer for 15 minutes, or until the sauce has thickened slightly.

4 ADD the ground almonds and the chicken, along with any juices, to the pan and cook for 15 minutes, or until the chicken is cooked through and tender. Remove from the heat, stir in the yoghurt and coriander and season well. Serve with steamed basmati rice.

SERVES 4.

Chicken mole

2 onions

10 cloves garlic

1 chicken cut into 8 pieces

6 sprigs of fresh thyme

6 sprigs of fresh oregano

6 sprigs of fresh parsley

6 whole black peppercorns

6 whole dried mulato chillies

4 whole dried pasilla chillies

1/2 small chipotle chilli

1/4 cup (40 g) raisins

1/4 cup (40 g) sesame seeds

400 g can peeled Italian tomatoes

1 tablespoon dried oregano

1/2 teaspoon ground allspice

1 slice of day-old white toast bread, crust removed

2 cloves

1 teaspoon cumin seeds

1 teaspoon coriander seeds

2 tablespoons canola oil

1 tablespoon tomato paste

1 cinnamon stick

1/4 teaspoon sugar

20 g Mexican chocolate, chopped

1/2 cup (25 g) finely chopped fresh coriander leaves

TOASTING the dried chillies draws out the flavour, but be careful not to burn them as they will become bitter.

1 CUT 1 onion into quarters, and 4 cloves of garlic into slices, and place in a large saucepan with the chicken pieces, thyme, oregano, parsley and peppercorns. Cover with cold water, add 1 teaspoon of salt and bring to the boil. Reduce the heat and simmer for 20–25 minutes, or until the chicken is cooked through and tender. Reserve 1 cup (250 ml) cooking liquid.

2 CUT open the chillies, discarding the stems, seeds and membranes. Toast carefully for 20 seconds in a hot frying pan, then transfer to a bowl. Cover with 3 cups (750 ml) boiling water and soak for 15 minutes. Soak the raisins in hot water for 20 minutes, then drain. Toast the sesame seeds until golden.

3 BLEND the tomatoes, with their juice, in a food processor until smooth. Add the oregano, allspice, bread, raisins, sesame seeds, and chillies with their soaking water, and blend until smooth. Strain, pressing the liquid through the sieve. Reserve the liquid and discard the pulp. In a small frying pan over low heat, dry-fry the cloves and cumin and coriander seeds for 1–2 minutes, or until fragrant. Grind to a fine powder in a mortar and pestle or a spice grinder.

4 FINELY dice the remaining onion and crush the remaining garlic. In a heavy-based frying pan, large enough to fit all the chicken pieces in one layer, heat the canola oil over medium heat. Cook the onion and garlic for 5 minutes. Add the ground spices and stir for 1–2 minutes, or until fragrant. Add the tomato paste, stir for 2 minutes, then add the tomato mixture, cinnamon stick and sugar. Cook over low heat for 20 minutes. Add the chocolate and the reserved cooking liquid from the chicken. Bring to a simmer, and add the chicken. Cook, covered, over low heat for 30 minutes. The chicken should be very tender and the sauce thick enough to coat the back of a wooden spoon. Stir in the coriander. Season well and serve with white rice and tortillas.

SERVES 6.

THE spices are sautéed with the onion and garlic before adding the liquid so their flavour becomes mellow and fragrant.

THE bread is added to the sauce to soak up liquid, giving the sauce a thicker and smoother texture

MEXICAN chocolate has a distinctive flavour and makes all the difference to this dish. Dark, bitter chocolate can be used instead.

MOLE is a traditional spiced Mexican sauce, varying in flavour and heat from region to region. The differences are due to the type of chilli used, but all share the slight bitterness of the Mexican chocolate.

COCONUT cream is extracted from the flesh of fresh coconuts to give a rich, thick cream.

THE delicious result in this green chicken curry is a perfect balance of hot, sour, salty and sweet flavours, a traditional combination in the cuisine in many southeastern parts of Asia.

COCONUT milk is taken from the coconut flesh after the cream has been pressed out. It has a much thinner consistency.

PALM sugar is made from the concentrated sap of various palm trees. It is available from Asian grocery stores.

YOU can refrigerate leftover curry paste in an airtight container for up to 2 weeks, or freeze in ice-cube trays for 2 months.

Green chicken curry

Fresh green chillies, galangal, lemon grass and spices are the base for the curry paste used in this popular Thai-style meal.

CURRY PASTE
1 teaspoon cumin seeds
1 teaspoon coriander seeds
1/4 teaspoon white peppercorns
2 stems lemon grass, white tender hearts only, chopped
10 long fresh green chillies, trimmed
3 cloves garlic, roughly chopped
5 cm x 2 cm piece fresh galangal or ginger, peeled and chopped
6 red Asian shallots, roughly chopped
5 fresh coriander roots
2 teaspoons shrimp paste
1/2 teaspoon ground black pepper
1 teaspoon grated lime rind
1 tablespoon lime juice

1 tablespoon fish sauce
1 cup (250 ml) thick coconut cream
750 g chicken thigh fillets, cut into thin strips about 1.5 cm thick
125 g snake beans, cut into 3 cm lengths
150 g broccoli, cut into small florets
100 g bamboo shoots, cut into thick strips
4 fresh kaffir lime leaves
2 cups (500 ml) coconut milk
1 tablespoon shaved palm sugar
2–3 tablespoons fish sauce
1/2 cup (30 g) fresh basil

1 FOR the curry paste, heat a small frying pan, add the cumin and coriander seeds and peppercorns and shake the pan over low heat for 1–2 minutes, or until aromatic. Transfer to a spice grinder or mortar and pestle and grind to a fine powder. Put in a food processor with the remaining paste ingredients and 1/4 teaspoon of salt and blend to a smooth paste. Transfer to a ceramic or glass bowl, cover tightly (or it will taint everything in the fridge) and refrigerate.

2 POUR the coconut cream into a wok or heavy-based saucepan, bring to the boil and cook over high heat for 10 minutes, or until it 'cracks', which means the oil separates. This helps thicken the sauce. Reduce the heat to medium, stir in half the curry paste and cook for 2–3 minutes, or until fragrant.

3 ADD the chicken and cook for another 3–4 minutes, or until almost cooked. Stir in the beans, broccoli, bamboo shoots, lime leaves and coconut milk. Bring to the boil, then reduce the heat and simmer for 4–5 minutes, or until the beans are cooked but still firm to the bite. Stir in the palm sugar, fish sauce and basil. Serve with rice and garnish with extra basil if desired.

SERVES 4–6.

Chicken and leek pies

Perfect for casual entertaining, these pies can be prepared in advance right down to the glazing of the pastry. Keep in the fridge, then pop them in the oven when your guests arrive.

2 tablespoons olive oil

500 g chicken thighs, cut into 2 cm dice

60 g butter

1 medium leek, finely sliced

3 cloves garlic, crushed

1/4 cup (60 ml) dry white wine

2 tablespoons plain flour

1 cup (250 ml) white chicken stock from page 14

1/2 cup (125 ml) cream

2 teaspoons chopped fresh thyme

2 tablespoons chopped fresh parsley

2 sheets butter puff pastry

1 egg, lightly beaten

SLOW cooking of the leek and garlic is very important to mellow the flavours and enhance the sweetness of the leeks.

1 HEAT the olive oil in a heavy-based frying pan and cook the chicken in two batches over high heat for 3–4 minutes each batch, until lightly browned but not cooked all the way through. Remove from the pan with a slotted spoon.

2 MELT the butter in the same pan and cook the leek and garlic over low heat for 6–8 minutes, or until soft. Return the chicken to the pan. Add the wine and boil for 2–3 minutes, or until nearly all the wine has evaporated. Sprinkle the flour over the top, stir for 1 minute, then add the stock, cream and thyme. Reduce the heat and simmer gently for 20 minutes, or until the chicken is tender and the sauce has reduced and thickened. Season to taste, remove from the heat and cool. Stir in the parsley.

3 PREHEAT the oven to moderately hot (200°C/400°F/Gas 6). To make individual pot pies, divide the mixture among four 1¼ cup (315 ml) ramekins. Cut four 12 cm rounds from the pastry, brush the ramekin rims with a little beaten egg, then place the pastry lids on top. Press the rims down firmly to seal. Cut out the pastry scraps if you wish and decorate the tops, brush with egg and cut three steam holes in each pie with a sharp knife. Bake on the bottom shelf for 15–20 minutes, until the pastry is golden.

SERVES 4.

TO make one large pie, place the mixture in a shallow 23 cm pie dish, roll the two sheets of pastry together and place over the mixture. Seal the edges with a fork. Make several small steam holes in the pastry with a sharp knife. Brush with beaten egg and bake in a moderate (180°C/350°F/Gas 4) oven for 30–35 minutes, or until golden. Turn the page for more pie filling suggestions.

IT is easier to work with the puff pastry while it is still partially frozen, especially if it is a warm day.

IT is important to cook out the wine until nearly evaporated or the wine will dominate the subtle flavour of the vegetables.

GLAZING the pastry with egg gives it a golden glow when cooked. It also helps to form a seal around the pie.

PIE mixture is ideal for freezing in individual portions in zip-lock bags. Keep pastry on hand in the freezer and you have all the makings for a quick and tasty meal.

pie fillings

chicken and mushroom

FOLLOW the recipe for Chicken and leek pies, but add 150 g sliced
Swiss brown mushrooms to the pan, after the leek has softened,
and cook for another 6–8 minutes before adding the wine to the pan.
Omit the thyme and add 1 tablespoon of finely chopped sage with
the parsley. Proceed with the recipe.

chicken and vegetable

FOLLOW the recipe for Chicken and leek pies, adding 1 diced carrot
and 1 diced celery stick to the pan with the leek. Cook for another
5–6 minutes, then add 1/2 cup (80 g) frozen peas, cook for 2 minutes
and then proceed with the recipe.

curried chicken

FOLLOW the recipe for Chicken and vegetable pies, but add
2 tablespoons hot Indian curry powder when adding the carrot and
celery. Cook for 5–6 minutes, then add the frozen peas and cook
for 2 minutes. Leave out the thyme and use $1/2$ cup (30 g) chopped
fresh coriander instead of the parsley. Proceed with the recipe.

sour cream and tarragon

FOLLOW the recipe for Chicken and leek pies, but omit the cream and
thyme. When the chicken is tender, transfer 3 tablespoons of the
sauce to a small bowl and add $1/2$ cup (125 g) sour cream and
1 tablespoon chopped fresh tarragon. Stir well to combine, then
mix in with the rest of the pie filling. Proceed with the recipe.

FRESH oregano, rosemary or thyme can be used instead of the herbs used here. Fresh herbs taste much better than dried in a stuffing.

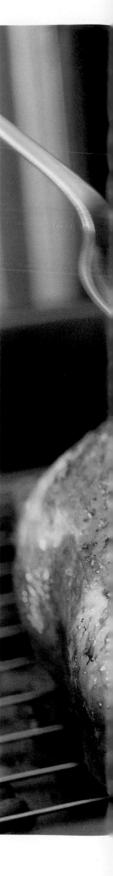

OTHER delicious stuffings are shown on pages 90–91. If you prefer, you can just season the inside of the chicken and stuff it with some fresh herbs.

TRUSSING the chicken keeps it in a neat shape and holds in the filling. Some people use long, metal skewers pushed through the skin, instead of string.

RUBBING butter all over the skin adds flavour to the chicken, as well as transforming the skin into an appealing golden crust.

ALTHOUGH some cooks recommend turning the chicken over during cooking, this isn't necessary, and is quite difficult. It is best to cook with the breast facing upwards.

The perfect roast chicken

The distinctive aroma of a chicken roasting in the oven sends the taste buds into overdrive. Serve with your favourite roasted vegetables.

60 g butter, softened
1 small onion, finely chopped
150 g soft white breadcrumbs
2 tablespoons chopped fresh parsley
1 tablespoon chopped fresh tarragon
2 teaspoons grated lemon rind
2 cups (500 ml) brown chicken stock
   from page 16
1.6–2 kg chicken
1 large onion
1 carrot
2 celery sticks
1 tablespoon plain flour

1 MELT 25 g of the butter in a saucepan over low heat and just before it starts to foam, add the onion and fry gently, stirring occasionally, for 5–8 minutes, until soft and golden.

2 WHILE the onion is cooking, combine the breadcrumbs, parsley, tarragon and lemon rind in a bowl. Season to taste.

3 ADD half the stock to the onion and bring to the boil. Pour it over the breadcrumb mixture and stir to combine well. Allow the mixture to cool completely. Never stuff a chicken with warm or hot stuffing as this increases the risk of salmonella developing.

4 PAT the inside of the chicken dry with paper towels. Using clean hands, fill the cavity of the chicken with the cold stuffing. Just fit it in neatly, not too too tightly, because the stuffing expands during cooking and will burst out if too firmly packed.

5 TRUSS the chicken. To do this, use a 90 cm piece of kitchen string, tie both chicken legs together, twisting the string around a couple of times. Run the string around the thighs and under the wings on both sides of the bird, then pull it tightly and tie a firm knot at the neck. Trim off any excess string. Alternatively, you can use a shorter length of string and just tie the two legs closer together. Any excess skin at the neck of the bird can be tucked under the wings.

6 PREHEAT the oven to moderately hot 200°C (400°F/Gas 6). Spread the remaining butter over the skin of the chicken, then season well with sea salt and pepper. Place the chicken with the breast-side up on a roasting rack (see below), then prepare the vegetables.

7 CHOP the vegetables into large chunks, not too small, otherwise they will burn before the chicken is cooked and you will end up with a bitter gravy. Spread the vegetables in the base of a sturdy roasting tin. Place the chicken, on its rack, over the vegetables and roast for 45 minutes. Remove from the oven, tilt the tin slightly and scoop up the buttery juices to baste the chicken. Return to the oven and roast for another 30 minutes.

8 REMOVE the chicken from the oven and test to see if it's done by piercing through the lower part of the thigh with a skewer. If the juices run clear, it is cooked, but if not, return it to the oven for another 10–15 minutes. Cover loosely with foil if browning too quickly. Leave the chicken to rest while you prepare the gravy.

9 REMOVE the vegetables from the roasting tin with a slotted spoon and discard. Spoon all but 3 tablespoons of the fat from the roasting tin, then place the tin on the stove top. Stir in the flour and cook for 1 minute, until it starts to brown. Scrape the crusty bits from the base. Add the remaining chicken stock and cook for 3–4 minutes. Add any juices that may have come out of the chicken while resting. Strain the gravy through a sieve and keep it warm. If you like a very glossy gravy, whisk 20 g of cold butter into the gravy just before straining.

SERVES 4–6.

ROASTING RACKS There are several types you can use. One is a 'V' shape that cradles the chicken well and helps brown the skin evenly. A vertical rack holds the chicken well, but is not suitable for large birds. Any sort of flat rack that is used for baking or cooling can also be used.

USING a wooden spoon, scrape the sediment from the bottom of the pan. It contains most of the flavour for the gravy.

STEADY the chicken with a carving fork. A sharp, heavy knife will make carving easier, and will stop you tearing the flesh.

RESTING t
and succul

...hicken after roasting and before carving allows the juices to be absorbed back into the chicken meat. This results in a more tender ...hicken and also makes it easier to carve.

stuffings for roast chicken

chicken liver stuffing

MELT 50 g butter in a small frying pan, add 1 finely chopped onion and 6 chopped bacon rashers, then cook for 5 minutes, or until the onion is golden. Allow to cool. Process 120 g fresh white bread, crusts removed, in a food processor with the onion, bacon, 2 tablespoons each of fresh sage and parsley, and 1 tablespoon fresh thyme, until finely chopped. Add 2 chicken livers, trimmed of excess fat and sinew, and process for a few seconds (don't overprocess). Transfer to a bowl, then fold in 1 egg. Season with salt and pepper. Make sure the mixture is completely cold before stuffing your chicken.

parsley, parmesan and lemon stuffing

PROCESS 120 g grated Parmesan, 50 g fresh flat-leaf parsley, zest of 2 lemons, 1/4 cup (60 ml) lemon juice, 150 g fresh white breadcrumbs and 1 egg in a food processor to just combine. Don't overprocess. Moisten with 2 tablespoon virgin olive oil. Season with salt and pepper.

couscous stuffing

PUT 110 g instant couscous in a bowl. Put $^1/_4$ cup (60 ml) orange juice in a heatproof jug and add boiling water to bring up to $^2/_3$ cup (170 ml). Pour over the couscous and leave for 15 minutes. Run a fork through the couscous to break up all the lumps, then season with salt and pepper. Heat 2 teaspoons oil in a small frying pan, add 1 finely chopped onion and cook for a few minutes until softened but not coloured. Add 1 teaspoon ground cumin and $^1/_2$ teaspoon each of ground coriander and ground cinnamon. Heat for 30 seconds, then add to the couscous. Chop 50 g each of dried apricots and dried figs into small pieces and add to the couscous with the zest of an orange, 25 g toasted pine nuts, 25 g shelled pistachios and 20 g chopped fresh flat-leaf parsley. Mix well and cool completely before stuffing your chicken.

rice and nut stuffing

ADD 50 g wild rice to a saucepan of cold, salted water. Bring to the boil, simmer for 10 minutes, then add 200 g basmati rice and cook for 15 minutes. While the rice is cooking, bring $^1/_4$ cup (60 ml) orange juice to the boil in a small saucepan and add 100 g dried cranberries. Turn off the heat and leave to soak for 15 minutes. Drain the rice under cold water, then cool. Transfer to a bowl, then add the cranberries, $^1/_2$ teaspoon ground cinnamon, 100 g roasted, roughly chopped macadamias, 50 g shelled pistachios, 2 teaspoons chopped fresh rosemary and the zest of 1 large orange. Season well. Stir 20 g melted butter through the mixture, then cool before using.

Roast chicken with butter under the skin

In this recipe, butter flavoured with garlic and herbs is pushed under the skin, resulting in wonderfully juicy flesh, brimming with aroma and flavour.

3 teaspoons olive oil
1.6–2 kg chicken
140 g unsalted butter, softened
2 small cloves garlic, crushed
1½ tablespoons chopped fresh parsley
1½ tablespoons chopped fresh French tarragon

1 PREHEAT the oven to moderately hot (190°C/375°F/Gas 5). Use the oil to rub into your fingers to help ease the skin from the chicken. Using your index and middle finger, gently ease the skin away from the flesh, being careful not to break the skin. You may find you need to exert a little more pressure at the top or use a small knife to disconnect the skin in that area. All the breast skin should now be loose.

2 PLACE 80 g of the butter in a small bowl, add the crushed garlic and the herbs, then season with salt and pepper. Work the butter under the skin so that it covers all the breast meat. Pat the skin back in place. Use the remaining butter to spread all over the outside of the bird. Season with salt and pepper.

3 PLACE the chicken on a rack over a shallow roasting tin and pour 1 cup (250 ml) water into the tin. Roast for 1 hour to 1 hour 15 minutes. If the breast begins to darken when cooking, cover with foil, then uncover for the last 15 minutes of cooking. Allow the chicken to rest for 15 minutes before carving it.

SERVES 4–6.

THERE is a variety of flavoured butters on the next page, or feel free to experiment with a mixture of your favourite herbs and spices.

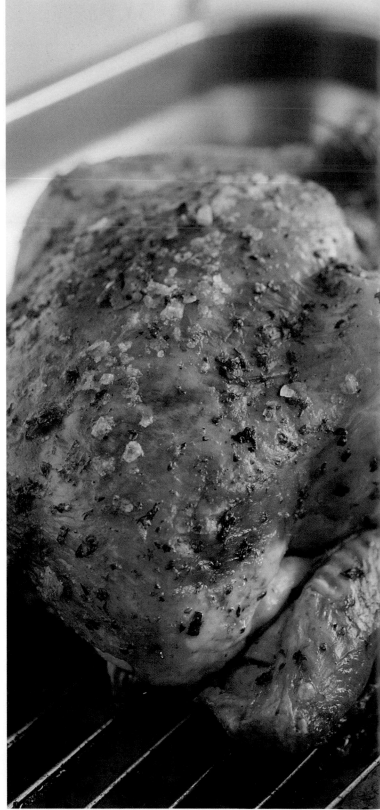

IF you like, you can stuff the chicken using one of the stuffings on pages 90–91. If so, it may take a little longer for the chicken and stuffing to cook through.

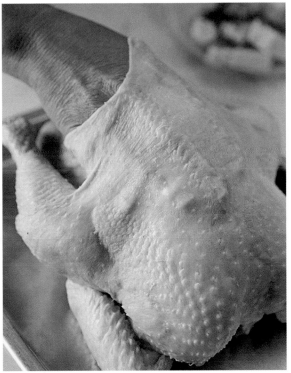

IF you are preparing a larger bird using this method you may have to use scissors or a small knife to disconnect the skin from the flesh.

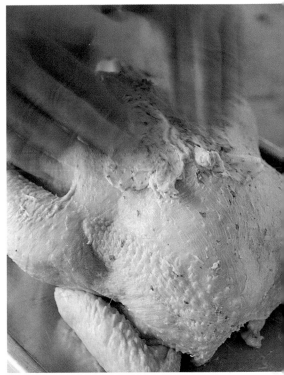

THE butter will adhere more easily to the skin if you pat the chicken dry before you start.

ADDING water to the roasting tin prevents the drippings from burning and creating smoke in the oven.

REST the chicken before carving so that the juices redistribute and settle evenly, resulting in moist chicken throughout.

CHOOSE heads of garlic that are firm and hard. Any soft or discoloured patches will taste rancid and spoil the flavour of the dish.

CHOP the rosemary finely before adding it to the dish. Whole rosemary leaves are so firm and pungent, they are rather unpleasant to eat.

THE garlic cloves only need a little colouring at this point, so cook them over medium heat for just 2–3 minutes before adding the chicken.

COVERING the casserole lid with a double layer of foil ensures that no steam can escape, locking in all the juices and flavours.

Chicken with forty cloves of garlic

Don't be alarmed by the amount of garlic in this dish. Cooked in this way, the garlic becomes sweet and tender. Serve with mashed potato.

20 g unsalted butter
1 tablespoon extra virgin olive oil
1.6 kg chicken
40 cloves garlic (preferably young), unpeeled
1½ tablespoons finely chopped fresh rosemary
1 bouquet garni (1 sprig thyme, 2 bay leaves,
   2 sprigs parsley)
300 ml dry white wine
100 ml white chicken stock from page 14

1 PREHEAT the oven to moderately hot (200°C/400°F/ Gas 6). Place a medium casserole on the stovetop, add the butter and oil and, when it starts to foam, add the chicken and brown for 5 minutes each side. Remove the chicken.

2 ADD the garlic cloves to the casserole and cook until they just start to take on some colour. Add the rosemary and bouquet garni, return the chicken to the casserole dish, then pour in the wine and stock. Season well with salt and black pepper and bring to a gentle simmer. Put the lid on the casserole, then cover with two layers of aluminium foil. Place in the oven and cook for 1 hour.

3 REMOVE the casserole dish from the oven, take off the foil and lid, then return to the oven for 15 minutes to brown the skin. Take the chicken out of the casserole and leave it to rest for 10 minutes.

4 PLACE the casserole on the stovetop and simmer the sauce until it has reduced to about 1 cup (250 ml). Remove the bouquet garni.

5 CARVE the chicken and serve on mashed potato with a little of the sauce and some garlic cloves. The idea is to squash the cloves into the sauce to enhance the flavour.

SERVES 4–6.

WHEN the dish has finished cooking, the idea is for each person to squash the roasted garlic cloves into the sauce to enhance the flavour.

Roasted lemon chicken pieces

The beauty of this dish lies in its simplicity. Once the aromas have filled your kitchen, it will no doubt become a mainstay.

1/2 cup (125 ml) lemon juice
1 teaspoon finely chopped lemon zest
3 cloves garlic, crushed
1 tablespoon chopped fresh thyme
2 tablespoons chopped fresh parsley
1/4 cup (60 ml) olive oil
1/2 teaspoon freshly ground black pepper
1.5 kg chicken, cut into 10 pieces

1 IN a large shallow glass or ceramic dish, mix together the lemon juice, lemon zest, garlic, thyme, parsley, olive oil and ground pepper. Add the chicken pieces and turn them until they are coated in the marinade. Cover and refrigerate for 8 hours, turning in the marinade occasionally.

2 PREHEAT the oven to moderately hot (200°C/400°F/ Gas 6). Remove the chicken from the marinade and lightly season with salt. Place in a roasting tin in a single layer so the dish is not overcrowded. Roast for 40 minutes, or until cooked through. Serve piled on a platter and drizzle with the cooking juices from the pan.

SERVES 4.

USE a good-quality olive oil, which, when combined with the cooking juices from the pan, will make a delicious sauce. Serve with crusty bread or mashed potato.

SQUEEZE your own lemon juice as the flavour is far superior to the commercially available ready-squeezed juices.

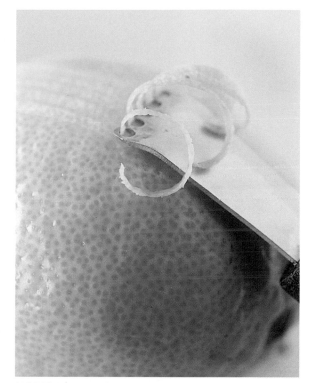

USING a zester is the easiest way to zest a lemon, but you can also use a vegetable peeler. Make sure you remove the bitter white pith before using.

ALMOST any herb would be suitable for this recipe. For example, try using parsley, mint, rosemary, sage, basil or majoram.

CERAMIC or glass dishes are best for marinating. Metal reacts with acids, such as lemon juice, used in marinades, and plastic absorbs strong flavours.

MAKE sure you drain off the excess beaten egg so that the crumbs stick to the chicken but do not become soggy.

FOR an Asian variation to the crumb flavour, use coriander, mint, lime rind and chilli powder instead of the parsley, lemon rind and cayenne.

BUTTERMILK is a low-fat milk that has been fermented slightly to give it its characteristic sour flavour.

TO ensure that the oil stays hot enough, don't overcrowd the pan. The chicken pieces shouldn't touch one another.

THESE chicken pieces are also delicious served cold and are perfect to pack up and take on a picnic lunch.

Deep-fried crumbed chicken pieces

When chicken pieces are thoroughly coated before deep-frying, the coating forms a seal that turns crispy while keeping the inside flesh tender and juicy.

1.5 kg chicken, cut into 10 pieces
$^3/_4$ cup (140 g) ground almonds
3 cups (240 g) fresh white
   breadcrumbs
1 tablespoon finely chopped
   fresh parsley
1 teaspoon grated lemon rind
$^1/_2$ cup (60 g) plain flour
$1^1/_4$ teaspoons cayenne pepper
2 teaspoons onion powder
2 teaspoons garlic powder
2 eggs
canola oil, for deep-frying
lemon wedges, for serving

RANCH DRESSING
1 small clove garlic, crushed
$^3/_4$ cup (185 g) mayonnaise
$^1/_2$ cup (125 ml) buttermilk
2 tablespoons finely chopped
   fresh parsley
1 tablespoon finely chopped
   chives
$1^1/_2$ teaspoons lemon juice
$1^1/_2$ teaspoons Dijon mustard
1 teaspoon onion powder

1 PAT the chicken dry with paper towels. Mix the almonds, breadcrumbs, parsley and lemon rind on a plate. Season the flour with cayenne pepper, onion powder, garlic powder and salt on another plate. Beat the eggs together in a bowl.

2 PRESS the chicken pieces into the flour, then dip in the egg and finally the breadcrumbs, making sure that each piece is well coated. Refrigerate the crumbed chicken for 30 minutes.

3 FOR the ranch dressing, in a small bowl or mortar and pestle, mash together the garlic and $^1/_4$ teaspoon salt until a paste is formed. Add the mayonnaise, buttermilk, parsley, chives, lemon juice, Dijon mustard and onion powder, and whisk together. Season well, cover and leave in the refrigerator for at least an hour before serving to allow the flavours to blend and develop.

4 PREHEAT the oven to moderate (180°C/350°F/Gas 4–6). Pour enough oil into a saucepan or deep-fryer to ensure the chicken will be completely covered. Heat the oil to 160°C (315°F) or until a cube of bread browns in 30–35 seconds. Using tongs, carefully lower the chicken in batches into the oil and cook for 8–10 minutes, or until golden brown, crisp and cooked through. The thigh and drumstick pieces will take longer to cook than the breast pieces. Drain on paper towels and keep warm in the oven while you cook the rest. Serve with ranch dressing and lemon wedges.

SERVES 4.

Chicken Kiev

This classic Continental dish has fallen out of fashion in recent years but, like all good things, it deserves to be rediscovered.

125 g unsalted butter, softened
4 cloves garlic, finely chopped
1 tablespoon finely chopped fresh parsley
1/2 teaspoon dried tarragon
1/2 teaspoon finely grated lemon rind
4 chicken breasts with first joint of wing attached, skinned
    and boned, tendorloin removed (about 160 g each)
2 eggs
1/2 cup (60 g) plain flour
3 cups (300 g) dried breadcrumbs
sunflower or mild-flavoured peanut oil, for deep-frying

1 BEAT the butter, garlic, parsley, tarragon and lemon rind in a bowl, using a wooden spoon, until soft and well blended. Push into a piping bag fitted with a plain nozzle.

2 PLACE the chicken breasts on a board and, with a sharp knife and starting at the thickest end of the fillet, cut a hole to form a pocket. Don't cut right through to the other end. Carefully pipe in just enough flavoured butter to fill the hole (don't overfill it or the filling will burst out during cooking). Refrigerate the breasts for 30 minutes.

3 LIGHTLY beat the eggs in a bowl. Spread the flour on a plate and the breadcrumbs on another. Dip each breast in the flour, then the egg and then the breadcrumbs. Repeat with the egg and breadcrumbs. Make sure the breasts are completely covered. Chill the breasts while you heat the oil.

4 POUR enough oil into a deep-fryer or saucepan to ensure the breasts will be completely covered. Heat the oil to 160°C (315°F) or until a cube of bread browns in 30–35 seconds. Using tongs, carefully lower the chicken into the oil, cooking two at a time, for about 5 minutes, until they are cooked through and golden. Serve immediately.

SERVES 4.

CHICKEN Kiev can also be pan-fried, if you prefer. Heat a little oil and butter in a pan, cook the breasts until golden on both sides, then finish in the oven until cooked through.

INSTEAD of parsley, you can use any fresh herbs for this recipe. Basil, chives or marjoram, for instance, would work well.

THE butter is much easier to mix until smooth if it has been allowed to soften first. If you have forgotten to leave it out, soften it in the microwave.

USING a piping bag to fill with breast with garlic butter is the easiest and cleanest method. If you don't have one, use a teaspoon instead.

AFTER removing the first batch of chicken, allow the oil to come back to the correct temperature before cooking the remaining breasts.

THE combination of spices and herbs blends to give the chicken its characteristic "southern" flavoured crust.

COATING the chicken pieces twice in the flour helps to produce a crisp, flavourful crust on the skin. As well as adding a wonderful texture, the crust also helps retain the moisture in the chicken.

RESTING the chicken pieces in the refrigerator after coating them helps to set the crust so it stays on during cooking.

Buttermilk southern fried chicken

This is a very popular dish in America, originating in the Deep South. Americans like to serve it with fluffy mashed potato.

1 tablespoon paprika
3 teaspoons salt (not sea salt)
1 teaspoon chicken stock powder
1 tablespoon garlic powder
2 teaspoons ground black pepper
1 tablespoon onion powder
2 teaspoons celery salt
1/4 teaspoon cayenne pepper
1 teaspoon dried oregano
1 teaspoon dried thyme
1 teaspoon dried basil

1/2 teaspoon dried sage
1 teaspoon ground white pepper
1 1/2 cups (375 ml) buttermilk
8 medium cloves garlic, crushed
1.5 kg chicken, cut into 10 pieces
 (or 1.5 kg chicken pieces on
 the bone)
1 1/2 cups (185 g) plain flour
corn oil, for deep-frying

THE enzymes in the buttermilk used in the marinade help tenderise the chicken, making the flesh moist and juicy when cooked.

1 IN a small bowl, combine the paprika, salt, chicken stock powder, garlic powder, black pepper, onion powder, celery salt, cayenne pepper, oregano, thyme, basil, sage and white pepper.

2 MIX together the buttermilk, garlic and 1 1/2 tablespoons of the spice mix in a shallow glass or ceramic dish. Add the chicken and stir around to coat well. Cover and marinate in the refrigerator for at least 24 hours.

3 IN another shallow bowl, mix the flour with the remaining spice mix.

4 WIPE the excess buttermilk from the chicken and dip in the flour mix to coat thoroughly. Place the chicken on a wire rack, and when you have finished coating all the chicken pieces, place each back in the flour and press the flour on firmly so there is a thick crust. Return to the wire rack and refrigerate for 1 hour to set the coating.

5 PREHEAT the oven to moderate (180°C/350°F/Gas 4). Fill a heavy-based saucepan one-third full of corn oil and heat to 160°C (315°F), or until a cube of bread dropped into the oil browns in 30–35 seconds. Cook the chicken in batches, without overcrowding the pan, for 8–10 minutes, until golden on all sides and cooked through. Remove with tongs and drain thoroughly on crumpled paper towels. Keep the chicken warm in the oven while frying the remaining pieces.

SERVES 4.

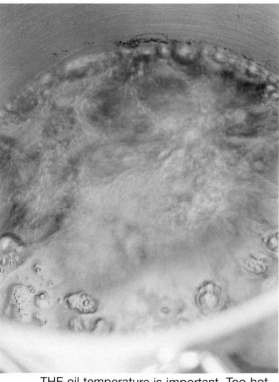

THE oil temperature is important. Too hot and the crust will burn before the chicken is cooked; too cool and it will absorb oil.

Honey chicken

Although not authentically Chinese, these crisp, sweet morsels served straight from the wok have long been a restaurant favourite.

1 kg boned chicken breasts, skin on
2¹/₂ tablespoons cornflour
1 cup (125 g) self-raising flour
1 egg, lightly beaten
peanut oil, for deep-frying, plus 1 tablespoon for stir-frying
1 tablespoon soy sauce
3 cm x 2 cm piece fresh ginger, finely chopped
¹/₃ cup (115 g) honey
2 spring onions, finely sliced on the diagonal, to garnish

1 CUT the chicken into small bite-sized pieces and put them in a bowl with 1¹/₂ tablespoons of the cornflour. Shake to coat well, then leave for 10 minutes.

2 IN a separate bowl, mix the flour and egg with 1¹/₄ cups (310 ml) cold water until you have a loose batter.

3 FILL a wok with enough oil to deep-fry the chicken, then heat to 190°C (375°F), or until a cube of bread dropped into the oil browns in 10 seconds. Dip the chicken pieces in the batter, allowing the excess to drip off, then fry the chicken in batches until crisp and golden. Drain on paper towels.

4 MIX the soy sauce and remaining cornflour in a small bowl.

5 DRAIN the oil from the wok and wipe the wok clean. Heat the remaining oil, add the ginger and stir-fry for 1 minute. Add the honey and, when it is heated through, add the chicken pieces and coat well. Add the soy and cornflour mixture and cook for 1 more minute.

6 PILE into a bowl or on a platter and garnish with the spring onion.

SERVES 4.

THIS sweet and crunchy chicken should be served straight away. It's delicious with steamed jasmine rice and stir-fried Asian greens.

THIS recipe works best with a mild-flavoured honey, such as clover. Honey made from scented flowers or trees will be too overpowering.

THE batter should just coat the chicken pieces. Allow the excess to drip off before deep-frying so the coating is light and crisp.

EXTREME care should be taken when deep-frying. Always make sure that your wok is stable before you begin cooking.

IT is important that the honey is very hot before adding the chicken. This means you can toss to coat quickly and the batter will stay crisp.

WHEN boning the wings, use a sharp knife and controlled movements. If you create a hole, use a toothpick to hold it together.

SERVE these chicken wings as an entrée or as part of a buffet. They can easily be converted into finger food — simply slice them into rounds and serve with a sweet chilli dipping sauce.

WHEN stuffing the wings, take care not to overfill them as the filling will expand during cooking and they may burst.

Stuffed chicken wings

12 large chicken wings
1 tablespoon kecap manis
1 tablespoon soy sauce
1/2 teaspoon sesame oil
1 teaspoon fresh fresh ginger
1 fresh red chilli, seeds and
    membrane removed, finely
    chopped
20 g dried rice vermicelli
50 g pork mince
300 g raw prawns, peeled and
    minced
1 teaspoon sugar

2 tablespoons fish sauce
2 spring onions, finely chopped
2 cloves garlic, crushed
1/2 cup (15 g) fresh coriander
    leaves, finely chopped
1 teaspoon lime juice
1/3 cup (60 g) rice flour
1/4 teaspoon onion powder
1/4 teaspoon garlic powder
peanut oil, for deep-frying

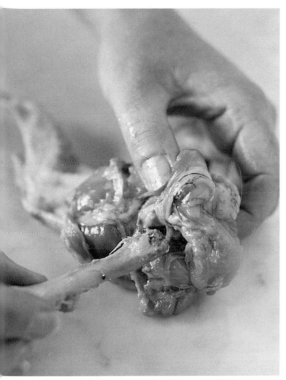

CAREFULLY rotate the bone until it dislodges from the socket, then you can simply pull it out.

WAIT until the chicken is cool enough to handle before proceeding with the drying and coating.

1 USING a small sharp knife and starting at the fatter end of the wing, scrape down along the bone, pushing the flesh and skin as you go, until you reach the joint. Twist and pull the bone away, push back the flesh, and cut around the joint, then carefully scrape down the two smaller bones, pushing back the flesh until you reach the second joint. Twist these bones from the socket and discard.

2 IN a shallow glass or ceramic dish, mix the kecap manis, soy sauce, sesame oil, ginger and chilli, add the chicken wings, and coat thoroughly in the marinade. Cover and refrigerate for at least 2 hours.

3 IN a bowl, soak the dried rice vermicelli in boiling water for 6–7 minutes to soften. Drain, cool and roughly chop.

4 IN a bowl, thoroughly combine the pork and prawn minces, sugar, fish sauce, spring onion, garlic, coriander, lime juice, vermicelli and 1/4 teaspoon each of salt and freshly ground black pepper. Divide into 12 even-sized balls.

5 REMOVE the wings from the marinade and scrape off any excess with a blunt knife. Fill the boned section of the wings with the filling (but don't overfill). Secure the top with a toothpick. Steam over boiling water for 8–10 minutes, then leave to cool slightly. Spread out on paper towels to absorb the moisture.

6 SEASON the rice flour with the onion and garlic powder and 1/4 teaspoon salt. Fill a wok or heavy-based saucepan one-third full of oil and heat to 180°C (350°F) or until a cube of bread dropped into the oil browns in 15 seconds. Coat the completely dry chicken wings in the seasoned rice flour, shaking off any excess. While still warm, deep-fry in batches for 6 minutes, or until golden and crisp. You may need to turn them with tongs to ensure even cooking. Drain on crumpled paper towels, and serve with sweet chilli sauce.

MAKES 12.

INDEX

Published by Murdoch Books®, a division of Murdoch Magazines Pty Limited,
GPO Box 1203, Sydney NSW 2001.

Managing Editor: Rachel Carter
Editor: Wendy Stephen
Creative Director: Marylouise Brammer
Designer: Michelle Cutler
Food Director: Jane Lawson
Food Editors: Vanessa Broadfoot, Christine Osmond
Recipe Development: Vanessa Broadfoot, Valli Little, Christine Osmond
Home Economists: Sonia Greig, Valli Little, Angela Tregonning
Photographer: Ashley Mackevicius
Food Stylist: Jane Hann
Food Preparation: Justine Poole

Chief Executive: Juliet Rogers
Publisher: Kay Scarlett
Production Manager: Kylie Kirkwood

National Library of Australia
Cataloguing-in-Publication Data.
How to cook chicken. Includes index.
ISBN 1 74045 138 4.
1. Cookery (Chicken). I. Title: Family circle
(Sydney, N.S.W.). (Series: Family circle step-by-step).
641.665
First printed 2002.
Printed by PMP PRINT.

Australian distribution to supermarkets and newsagents by
Gordon and Gotch Ltd, 68 Kingsgrove Road, Belmore, NSW 2192.
Distributed in NZ by Golden Press, a division of HarperCollins Publishers,
31 View Road, Glenfield, PO Box 1, Auckland 1.

INTERNATIONAL GLOSSARY OF INGREDIENTS

capsicum	red or green pepper	spring onion	scallion/shallot
coriander	cilantro	tomato paste (Aus.)	tomato purée, double concentrate (UK)
eggplant	aubergine	tomato purée (Aus.)	sieved crushed tomatoes/passata (UK)
snow peas	mangetout	zucchini	courgette